Trolling Truths

for Trout, Kokanee & Landlocked Kings

Comprehensive, current and revised

Sep & Marilyn Hendrickson

FAP

Frank Amato Publications

Trolling Truths
for Trout, Kokanee & Landlocked Kings

Comprehensive, current and revised

Sep & Marilyn Hendrickson

FAP

Frank Amato
Publications

ACKNOWLEDGEMENTS

Many folks have impacted our lives and we are eternally grateful. We had the opportunity to live and work in an environment that has been fun, challenging and profitable, and ended up making an impact on the sport of angling. How lucky is that! We spent 25 years developing, producing and marketing our line of SEP'S ultralight trolling products, and a few years ago, sold the business to young and enterprising folks who continue the legacy.

There will always be a special thank you to Les and Barbara Boyle, who in the beginning many years ago, took us fishing... all four of us in their 12-foot aluminum boat...and showed us how to catch fish in a lake. That is really how it began.

Then there are all the others...Tony Thiesson, Ed Rice, Bruce Wassom, Mike Campbell, Dan Miller, Tom Malmstadt, Ron & Lynn Gilliss, Bob Smalley, Leo

In the beginning, Les and Barbara Boyle.

Vrana, Blair Carpender, Richard Burton, Paul Burns, Scott Fordice, Bill Karr and the dearly departed Larry Green, to name just a few. We're fortunate to meet many amazing people in our travels and continue to make friends along the way.

These days we mostly associate with "cronies" – friends that continue to band together because we're so used to seeing each other, doing fun things and making great memories! Guess that's what comes with "old age"! We appreciate them all!

©2012 Sep and Marilyn Hendrickson
ALL RIGHTS RESERVED. No part of this book may be reproduced in any means (printed or electronic) without the written consent of the publisher, except in the case of brief excerpts in critical reviews and articles.

All inquiries should be addressed to:
Frank Amato Publications, Inc.
P.O. Box 82112 • Portland, Oregon 97282
www.amatobooks.com • (503) 653-8108

All photographs by the author unless otherwise noted
Illustrations: Tom Waters unless otherwise noted
Cover and book design: Tony Amato

SB ISBN-13: 978-1-57188-487-9   SB UPC: 0-81127-00332-7
Printed in China

1 3 5 7 9 10 8 6 4 2

CONTENTS

FOREWORD

"It's all in the presentation"
...whoever said it first, must have been an angler

Wе wrote the original "*Trolling Truths*" several years ago. The response has been terrific and we often hear from seasoned anglers who tell us they learned new tactics and techniques and we appreciate that very much. But it's the new devotees to the sport of fishing...the folks who are introducing their children to it, who matter the most. In our opinion, it's very important that youngsters get an opportunity to experience what

Andrew & Austin Erck with Great-grandpa Bud.

we already know, and if we can help to create that interest and love of the sport, it's time well spent. We want them to feel the excitement and adrenalin rush of "fish on"! That's why the update to the book, to keep it current and to provide pertinent information to folks so they get out, catch fish and pass on the fun part of "going fishing" to another generation.

If you enjoy catching rainbow trout, browns, cutthroat, mackinaw, kokanee and landlocked king salmon...this book is for you! It's mostly about trolling – the ultralight way, but we do deal a bit with other fish-catching techniques. Some chapters, mostly covering basics, remain somewhat the same as they were in Book One, but in many cases we have added more, as we continued to learn in our personal travels and angling adventures. Techniques, tactics and tackle might appear to be basic, but there's always something new...technology evolves...and the "how-tos" continue to progress, develop and change.

Anglers have trolled for years, using any and all systems, and they have been successful, some more than others. Trolling for fish is not rocket science, but doing it well is the goal. Properly utilizing new and innovative equipment and techniques can make a tremendous difference. Our equipment is light – our rods, reels, line and lures. We want to "feel the fight", each run, head-shake and tug of the fish, to maximize the fight of the fish and enjoy the moment.

As we began our journey, it was on the threshold of the development of technology and electronics which has certainly made a strong impact on fishing and the average angler. We were on the cutting edge of what was to come! We continue to refer to our lives as the "big bubble" and our friends and acquaintances know how thankful we are to be able to continue to do what we enjoy most.

We fish like you do. Some days are good, some great, and still others leave us wondering what could have been done differently. We want to emphasize...we're not experts, we're "experienced" and happen to have the opportunity to go fishing more than most folks.

This book shares our own expertise and experiences, but we surely do not profess to know it all. We are very quick to admit we continue to learn more every time we go fishing, and so should you!

INTRODUCTION

"The difference between a boat ride and fishing…is catching fish"

Primarily we troll. This offers the opportunity to cover more water or surface acres, thereby increasing the chances of locating more fish. It allows for the presentation of lures or bait right in the face of the fish, plus it provides a more natural presentation. Now, don't get this wrong…each year, monster fish are caught by bait dunkers, too. They catch their fair share of trophies, but trollers enjoy the challenge of unlocking the combination for hook-ups, using experience, judgment and a wide variety of ultralight equipment.

Trolling can be as simple as letting line and lure out behind the boat, or as complex as a melding of electronics, technology, experience and techniques.

Trolling involves idling the boat across the surface of the lake while placing offerings in the right place, at the right time, at the right depth, at the

right speed, with the right lure, in the right color, with the right action, and proper presentation. Sounds easy, doesn't it!

Angling success is not measured by doing most things right, but by doing everything right.

It is that mix of past experience, consistency of presentation plus knowledge, that routinely brings an angler great days of fishing. A myriad of high-tech electronics, such as global positioning systems, auto pilot steering, sonar locators, electronic downriggers, sidefinders, underwater cameras and more, are available to assist in catching more fish. However, be assured, anglers can find enhanced success by simply concentrating on the often overlooked BASICS of freshwater trolling.

Sep's Trolling Machine – Jetcraft Discovery 2025 Stingray.

It is as important to know where to fish as how to fish

First and foremost, an angler must be able to find the fish! This takes some thought and a little common sense. Every lake or reservoir has certain physical characteristics that attract fish. Knowing where and what to look for dramatically increases the chances of catching fish. Anglers should do their homework, starting by checking out key areas on a good-quality map.

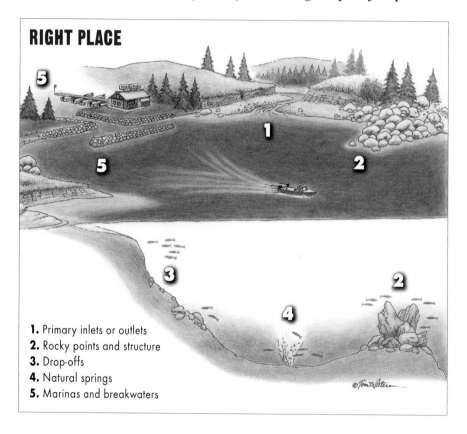

RIGHT PLACE

1. Primary inlets or outlets
2. Rocky points and structure
3. Drop-offs
4. Natural springs
5. Marinas and breakwaters

Primary Inlets and Outlets

One of the prime locations for trolling in a lake is within 100 to 200 yards of primary inlets and outlets. The cool, fresh waters of rivers, creeks and streams flow through the lake, bringing highly-oxygenated water and a broad spectrum of forage for trout and salmon to feed upon. Insects, aquatic life, minnows and small trout and salmon fry are but a few of the natural baits drawn downstream to a lake through its tributaries. Feeder streams, like primary inlets, and natural currents following the old river beds throughout the lakes, will bring abundant sources of food to the feeding fish waiting around these areas.

Dams, at the exit of lakes, act as primary outlets and the face of any dam will often provide large accumulations of fish. Natural currents will bring forage such as disoriented baitfish to the spillway and fish will definitely gather there. The area where a lake empties into a river or creek will certainly hold fish, waiting for an easy meal. Insects and other food sources float or drift on the surface or in the current toward the outlet. Large trout often hang out near outlets, slurping up anything edible floating past.

Rocky Points and Structure

These provide natural holding and feeding areas. Submerged islands, trees, old dams, bridges, brush piles and other structures all provide protection and are productive locations. The shape and structure of a lake and its points create natural pathways for fish. An enriched food chain is created in these rocky areas as aquatic life such as freshwater shrimp, leeches, emergers and minnows move among the rocks to feed on plankton and other forage. The organisms growing on and around rocky areas attract baitfish, which attract smaller game fish, which in turn attract larger game fish...and so on.

Drop-offs

Trout definitely like milling around the edges of drop-offs. They know that minnows hide and cruise in these areas, feeding and trying not to be fed upon, plus drop-offs offer them easy escape routes to deeper waters. Trollers working around drop-offs can often enjoy excellent action.

Natural Springs

Natural springs are found in many lakes, particularly in the volcanic regions of the West. These underwater springs bring a nearly continuous supply of fresh, highly-oxygenated water into the lake. In many cases, this water is warmer, or cooler, than that of the lake, and this often attracts huge schools of baitfish to these ideal condition areas. At times, the baitfish drawn to these locations can be so thick, they will signal a false bottom reading on a fish locator. Trout, kokanee and landlocked king salmon hang near these natural feeding grounds.

Marinas and Breakwaters

Just like in rocky areas, a food chain is established around marinas, boat docks and the rocks of breakwaters. Think about it, how many times have you seen huge schools of minnows around the pilings of a marina? Or, have you heard about or seen, big fish lurking under docks? Yes, there are definitely game fish around, trying for a quick and easy meal!

Research

Knowing where to find fish is half the battle in becoming a successful troller and doing research before heading out to an unfamiliar location will pay off. Carefully examine maps of the lake, looking for areas that may hold or support game fish. Check fishing newspapers and ask questions of local tackle shop and marina operators. They want you to catch fish, spread the word and return.

The Internet offers much...satellite views and topographical maps plus vast amounts of information on websites, in chat rooms and from state and federal agencies.

Often the quickest way to learn about a new body of water is to book an experienced, professional fishing guide. It is possible to learn in one day of fishing with a knowledgeable guide, as much as you would learn in several years on your own. If the guide is a quality guide... you should check referrals before booking...he will openly share tackle, baits, techniques, tactics and locations that will produce fish. The information you glean can save many hours of frustrating trolling time. After "picking" the guide's brain, you can easily apply the learned techniques when you head out on your own. The cost of a guide becomes minimal when compared to the time, expense and effort it would take to do it on your own.

Another tip

When wondering where to go on a lake...look for other boats. They will dot most every productive locale. If you have doubts about where to fish or how deep, don't hesitate to ask questions of passing anglers as they are generally a friendly bunch.

Another possibility, troll the same path the others are fishing. General courtesy dictates that you should not troll too closely to another boater and it is a good idea to keep at least a 30- to 50-yard buffer zone to avoid crossing over or tangling lines with fellow anglers. Valuable fish-catching time can be wasted while untangling lines or downriggers because of trolling too close to another boat or trolled offerings. It also makes the errant troller an unpopular member of the group, putting it mildly!

*One of the most common mistakes –
presenting offerings at the wrong depth*

Preciseness of presentation is key to angling success. Anglers often think they are trolling at the right depth, but can actually be off by a significant distance. It is important to troll offerings within the strike range of the quarry.

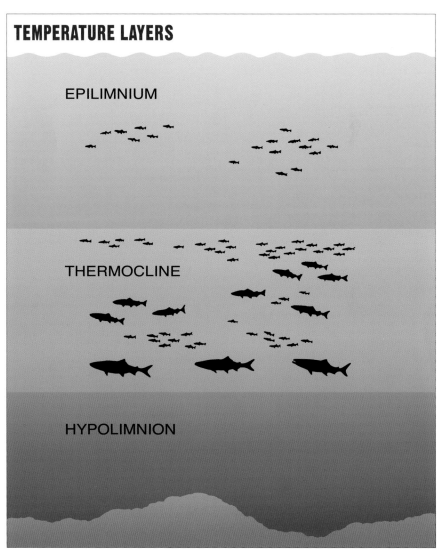

TEMPERATURE LAYERS

EPILIMNIUM

THERMOCLINE

HYPOLIMNION

Fish are cold-blooded. Their body temperature is the same as the surrounding water and every species of trout and salmon has a preferred temperature. Whenever this ideal temperature water is available to them, fish spend as much time as possible at that level. Trout and salmon species thrive in water, rich in oxygen, in the 52- to 58-degree range. This area, regardless of its depth, is known as the "thermocline". This is the area where fish will be most active and where they will be more willing to expend the energy required to chase and strike a lure or bait.

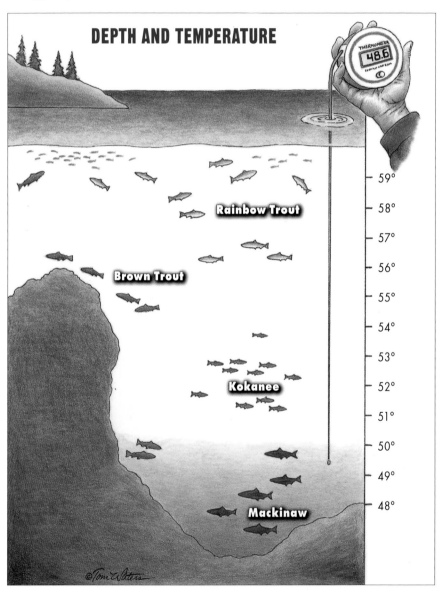

Marilyn with a 3-pound Eagle Lake trout.

Before attempting to intercept fish roaming below the surface, it is important to have a simple basic understanding of the make-up of the lake.

The upper layer of the lake is known as the "epilimnium". This layer contains an assortment of forage for trout and salmon, such as minnows, baitfish and aquatic insect life. The temperature and oxygen content of the epilimnium varies greatly, depending upon the season.

Immediately after ice out, the surface and shallow water along the shoreline attract fish searching for the first waters to be warmed by the rays of the sun. In the summer, the epilimnium is often warm, uncomfortable and too low in oxygen content for cold water species. Fish may venture into these warmer than preferred waters, especially in the early morning and late evening hours but normally they do not stay long. They prefer to live in the deeper, cooler waters of the lake's mid-range, known as the "thermocline". In the fall and early winter, weather and wind changes cause the surface and shallows to cool and become oxygenated, bringing game fish to the epilimnium layer of the lake, once again.

The thermocline is the nutrient and oxygen rich water of ideal temperature that is the summer home of coldwater species. For the most part, trout and salmon find themselves living in this concentrated ideal band of water, with perfect temperature and habitat, exactly where lures or bait need to be.

The lower level of the lake is known as the "hypolimnium". It is poor in oxygen and food supplies and offers little attraction to the fish. To put it simply ... it is a DEAD zone.

Preferred Temperature Ranges

Rainbow trout	55-58 degrees
Brown and brook trout	55-59 degrees
Mackinaw or lake trout	52-54 degrees
King salmon	52-54 degrees
Kokanee salmon	52-56 degrees

Finding the Thermocline

One of the most important pieces of equipment an angler should have in the tackle box, and one that very few do, is a water temperature thermometer. If used methodically and properly, a thermometer can provide information about proper trolling depth, and what color and type of lure to use. By testing and locating the upper and lower limits of the thermocline, an angler can find the exact depths to present offerings, whether trolling or stillfishing.

A wide variety of thermometers are available, ranging in cost, depending on how fancy an angler wants to get. Available for around $10, a tube thermometer can be attached and lowered on fishing line or, for a bit more, a digital gauge with cable and probe gives LED readouts on a small hand-held screen. A zealous angler can purchase a sensing unit on a dash-mounted screen that provides a digital readout of the temperature and speed at the downrigger ball. However, with today's improvements and innovations in electronic locators, fishfinders and GPS units, an angler can rely solely on them to find fish!

Watch the screen of the fish locator closely and make note of the depths at which fish are visible. Most fish locators on the market today provide clear pictures of what anglers are traveling over and can identify the proximity of the thermocline by indicating depths where fish are holding. It is important to learn to interpret and believe what the fish locator shows and a good idea to periodically re-check your manual to re-familiarize yourself with the basics of its operation. Keep learning till you have the confidence that what you see, you can interpret properly and understand what you are looking at. When available, take advantage of a class or two dealing with the intricacies of advanced updated fish locator instruction...this pays off big-time!

The thermocline can generally be identified by turning the sensitivity to maximum, then locating the colder denser water. The thermocline does not run at the same depths throughout the lake. By carefully watching the screen of the locator and adjusting depths as necessary, an angler can intercept the thermocline and greater numbers of cruising fish. For the most part, fish will be in the thermocline, but there are times they

Guide Cliff Spediacci with a trout caught trolling a grub in the thermocline.

do travel in and out of the band with frequency, especially when feeding heavily. Take the lake's temperature when traveling about to ensure that offerings are placed within or close to water of the ideal temperature range. Knowing the temperature at the depth where lures or bait are placed is definitely information an angler needs to know.

Guide Rick Kennedy with a great example of a "Mac".

There are a variety of ways of getting down

Adding lead weights, leaded keels or banana weights will certainly help get lures or baits down, but how far down do they go? The addition of weight is only guesswork at best and it comes between you and the fish. Even if a fish or two is caught, the troller is never really sure the correct depth has been reached and most likely the action would have been much better if the lure or bait had been precisely in the thermocline.

There are many charts and guidelines to help anglers determine actual depth when trolling with weights. The relationship between speed of the boat, lure drag and action, weight of line, length of leader line, wind and current direction will determine where or at what depth terminal offerings will run. There are far too many variables for an angler to accurately predict the true running depth of the lure.

Diving planes will take terminal offerings down...but just how accurate are they? Each such device has its own formula for line diameter and depth and it does get down...but to what depth? Keep the instructions that come with the original set-up as the many variables necessitate regular consultation! Diving devices do require the use of heavier tackle as they create an added strain on the rod, reel and line, which certainly interferes with the enjoyment of the fight.

Many years ago leadcore line revolutionized trolling, and there are still many advocates who continue to utilize this antiquated technique. Each thirty-foot section of line is a different color and a good rule of thumb, or guess, is for every color out, the line drops about five feet, if trolling one mph. Knowing the correct trolling speed is essential for accuracy and some varieties of line are designed to drop even deeper than the "five-feet-per color" standard. To intercept fish in a 40-foot thermocline, let out eight colors, placing the lure 240 feet behind the boat! This line is big and bulky and requires specialized tackle to handle the weight and size. Ask yourself, how deep does my leadcore line really drop? How fast am I trolling? Once again, guesswork at best.

The end result? To be able to catch more fish, get down with accuracy, down to the depth needed to intercept more fish! To ensure proper depth control and to eliminate guesswork, there is only one solution - downriggers!

*Sep setting
downrigger.*

*Scotty
downriggers
set for a hit.*

*Russ Faught
with record-
breaking
Flaming Gorge
kokanee.*

To get down accurately, you definitely need a downrigger

Downriggers are state-of-the-art in controlled depth fishing. To an angler, they can be the "secret to success" or a "nightmare of frustration". Downriggers, suitable to your needs, combined with a high-quality fish locator, provide a distinct advantage.

The most common mistake made when trolling is having terminal offerings at an unknown or incorrect depth. Some anglers simply hit the water and let out lines. Some anglers run lines on top and others end up scattering lines at varying depths. A myriad of devices are used to help get down, but just how deep is the lure, really? It is extremely important to know exactly how deep terminal tackle is running...fish can only look up, therefore, your terminal offerings must stay above the fish.

When summer temperatures warm our lakes, trout and salmon move to deeper waters in search of the thermocline and forage. Anglers using lead-core line, diving planes or heavy sinkers to get down, find these methods to be an inexact science at best. These techniques require the use of much heavier rods, reels and line...resulting in far less enjoyable experiences when fish are caught.

Downriggers are the most effective way to get lures to the proper depth.

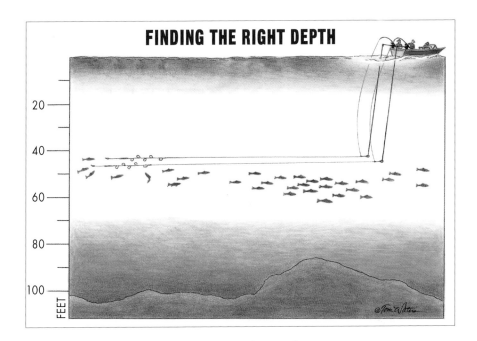

FINDING THE RIGHT DEPTH

Without a doubt, the single most effective way to get lures or bait accurately to the proper depth is to use downriggers. This method allows trollers to fish deep with light tackle and, most importantly, to enjoy the sport of fighting the fish. Too often heavier tackle means, "winching" in the fish, thereby eliminating enjoyment of the fight. To feel the fight – use ULTRALIGHT!

A downrigger is simply a reel-type device that takes line and lure down into the depths with accuracy and efficiency. The downrigger ball, or weight, is secured to the downrigger cable, to which a downrigger line release is attached. This takes fishing line and lure down to the desired depth. When a fish hooks up, the line is pulled free of the release, leaving the angler to fight the fish with no resistance.

At one time, downriggers were out of the price range of many anglers, but that is certainly not the case any longer. They were originally used in saltwater and heavy fresh-water applications, but current models are definitely practical for light line use. Manufacturers now make downriggers of high quality that fit any budget, with varying price points. There are even downriggers practical and efficient enough to bring along to clamp on rental boats, if desired.

The troller has many choices, from simple-to-operate hand-crank units to electronic computerized wonders that track the bottom of the lake and automatically raise and lower offerings. Or, an ingenious angler can simply take a length of rope or heavy line, mark off five-foot increments, attach a downrigger ball and release, clip on the fishing line and lower the basic "poor man's downrigger" over the side of the boat by hand!

The size or weight of the downrigger ball can vary, depending upon the application and the downrigger. Keep it light, and generally a six-pound ball is plenty for light trout and kokanee angling. When trolling slowly, water resistance is a concern and using a heavy ball is not necessary. When trolling in deep water or at faster speeds, a heavier, eight- or ten-pound ball works best, assuming the downrigger can hold such weight. The objective is to maintain accurate depth control by keeping the downrigger ball as straight down as possible, minimizing "blow-back" caused by drag in the water. The more cable that is out and the deeper the lure is, the greater the drag and blow-back.

When trolling with a downrigger, we recommend not holding the rod, but rather, placing it firmly in the rod holder, then "loading" it by tightening up line until the rod forms a graceful arc. When a fish hits and pops the line free from the release, the loaded up rod will take up slack line and semi-set the hook.

Proper use of downriggers is essential to a trolling angler's success. Downriggers are absolute necessities and should be used, as various situations warrant, from the surface to the lake's bottom. We run four top-of-the-line electric Scottys, two out the side and two off the stern.

Some seasoned anglers have enhanced the use of downriggers by adding a "dropper line", utilized for trolling two depths at the same time, on one fishing rod. This method consists of attaching a swivel to one end of a five-foot leader and a light-weight lure to the other. After the main line is connected to the downrigger re-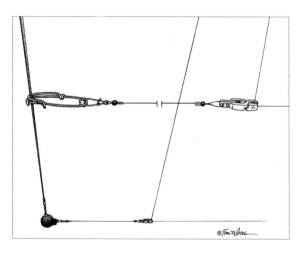lease and set at the desired depth, the swivel on the five-foot leader is attached to the main line and the lure end is tossed into the water toward the back of the boat.

As the angler trolls along, the lure will slowly sink below the surface and move to a point approximately half-way down – the apex of the bow in the line – to the downrigger ball. For example, if the downrigger is set at 40 feet deep, the dropper line will run near 20 feet, allowing the angler to attract more fish by covering two depths. If the only fish being caught are on the dropper line, then the downrigger is set too deep. Raise it up and try again, you might catch fish on both lines at the same time!

This method is very effective and can be used on any waters where downriggers are used. One thing that can frustrate the angler is the dropper line tangling with the main line when bringing in a fish. If this happens, simply cut the leader at the swivel, or lure, and pull it out. If another dropper line is tied and ready to go, the angler loses no fishing time.

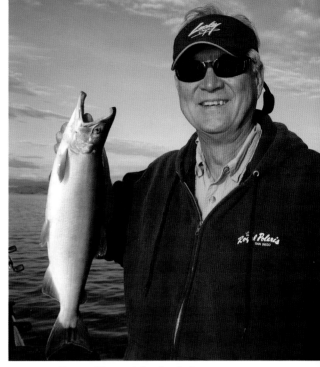

Larry Eng with nice kokanee caught downrigging.

The effectiveness of this technique quickly becomes obvious…it is easy to master and will certainly improve chances of catching fish.

The choice of a suitable "downrigger release" is also important. Many accessories of this type were originally geared for heavier applications and were difficult to attach, adjust and utilize. Manufacturers addressed this need and innovations hit the market. The Sep's release was designed to handle light-line needs easily and to dependably and smoothly release on the strike of a small to medium weight fish. The release can also be tripped with just a flip of the rod tip. Because of its simple "pinch" design, line can be easily inserted. The spring inside can be adjusted forward or backward to get a heavier or lighter release of line on the strike. The firm setting is very effective when using a heavier line or when the angler wants to control the line when it becomes free. The release has a wire leader with a snap for connecting it directly to the downrigger cable, or to the downrigger weight itself. The heaver super release has a firmer grip and is used for the ultra-small diameters of super lines.

The stacker is a "companion" device, to be used with a downrigger. This small metal clip allows the angler to troll two lines on one downrigger cable. Stackers make it possible to fish two different depths, off the same downrigger. Simply put out the first line as usual, attach the stacker to the downrigger cable, then attach the second line and send it all down.

5. DOWNRIGGER DYNAMICS

The importance of accurate depth control cannot be overstressed

Imagine the fish locator indicating several schools of nice-sized fish, holding suspended at the 40-foot mark, holding in 80 feet of water. You're trolling at a speed of one-half to one mile per hour, pulling a standard rigged flasher and lure. You have just let out line...the flasher rig is 100 feet behind the boat. You know fish are holding at 40 feet and quickly lower your offering. How deep would you lower it to intercept fish cruising at 40 feet? 40 feet...right? WRONG!

Here's the hitch! Allow for the natural drop of the terminal rig! Trolling flashers or dodgers, 100 feet behind the boat, can cause the terminal rig to drop as much as ten percent...from five to ten feet, depending upon trolling speed and size of flashers and lures being used.

By lowering the downrigger to 25 feet, the terminal flasher rig will be running at or near, 35 feet. This is five feet above the fish...within perfect attack range. Often trollers fail to take this into account and end up with the offerings well below the fish, subsequently striking out, time after time.

This is the SINGLE, BIGGEST mistake that anglers make.

Anglers must know exactly how deep lures and bait are in relation to the fish. It is critical to keep offerings above fish, preferably within a comfortable strike range of three to five feet. The eyes of fish are located near the top of their heads, enabling them to see silhouettes of bait upward, against the light surface. It is much better to have the lure or bait as much as twenty feet above the fish, rather than one foot below. Fish DO NOT look down!

Trout are likely to be spooked by downrigger weights and wire. They will move away from intimidating boat noise and approaching downrigger balls as the boat passes nearby or overhead. If "short-lining", that is, running a lure a short distance behind the boat, chances are you will pass by targeted fish and rarely have a hit. Think about it...you are using a six pound, or larger, downrigger ball. When this comes through or past a school of fish, they will definitely move off to the side. If the lure is right behind the downrigger ball, within ten feet or so, the spread out fish will miss the offering.

If you are after bigger, smarter, more wary trout, drop the offering back...way back. Greater success is found by disassociating terminal offerings, lures or bait, from the boat and engine noise. This can be done easily by keeping lures at least 100 feet behind the downrigger ball. The fish may still move out of the way of the ball, but will have adequate time to return to its original spot and may pursue the offering, once the weight

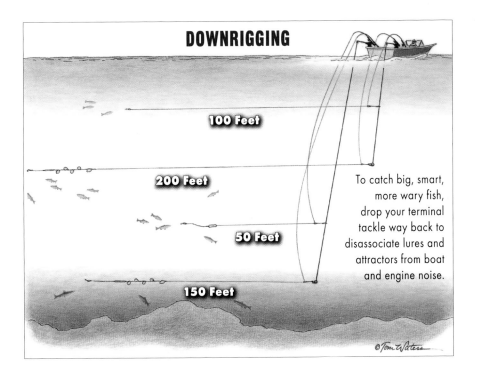

DOWNRIGGING

100 Feet

200 Feet

50 Feet

To catch big, smart, more wary fish, drop your terminal tackle way back to disassociate lures and attractors from boat and engine noise.

150 Feet

©Tom Waters

has passed by. At some lakes, fish are so finicky that a troller may need to let out 200 feet or more of line, to fool big, elusive trout. Remember...allow for the natural drop of terminal tackle.

There are times to down-rig deep and times to down-rig shallow. Cold weather and ideal water temperatures bring hungry trout to the surface to feed on minnows, baitfish and other insect and aquatic life that venture into the surface waters or shallow shorelines. Sub-freezing temperatures will cause moss and grasses to die and float to the surface, making top-lining tactics ineffective when weeds get picked up by lines every few minutes. To reduce the out-of-water, down-time action caused by having to clean lines, try this...using the downrigger, lower offerings to just below the surface at two to five feet. This tactic allows lures or bait to stay shallow, where the fish are, and the troller can continue top-line action without the constant interruption of clearing weeds from the line and terminal offerings.

Schooling fish, such as kokanee and landlocked king salmon, present a different scenario. These species are highly competitive for food sources and are not readily spooked by downrigger balls and cables. They will follow, pursue and strike offerings as close as three feet from the downrigger ball. When a school is located or a fish hooks up, it is a good idea to run tight turns back through the same area, staying in touch with the school. Short-lining ten to twenty feet behind the downrigger ball, enables anglers to

*Jared & Jesica Johnson with a
Flaming Gorge kokanee.*

"turn on a dime" and pass quickly back through the same school of fish, rather than making the wide sweeping turn of a "long-liner". Keep a close eye on the fish locator as schools of salmon may be found at different levels around the lake. Just because they are caught at 40 feet in one spot, does not mean the next school will be at that same depth.

Early-season kokanee or king salmon are found scattered about the lake with very little schooling activity and even though they do not easily spook with short lines, it is recommended that anglers long-line off the downrigger to best intercept these fish. Trolling with 75 to 100 feet of line behind the downrigger provides adequate time to make necessary depth adjustments for each scattered fish spotted on the locator. When passing over fish, adjust trolled offerings precisely, keeping lures or bait five feet above the fish. This method increases the odds of success by ensuring that as many scattered fish as possible get to see the trolled offerings.

As the season progresses into summer, salmon will be found in small schools of just a few fish at a time. By early fall, and before the spawn, salmon are found in schools of hundreds and often thousands of fish at a time. This is when the short-line, tight-turn technique really produces.

A kokanee bite is anything but consistent! One day it is wide open, the next day the bite is off…big time! The locator screen can light up, indicating

*Marilyn's rainbow,
caught trolling "way back".*

an abundance of fish and the depth at which they are holding, but getting a hit is always a challenge. The kokanee bite can start and stop, all day long. Periods of peak activity can be followed by lulls of up to an hour or more and then it's wide-open action again. Don't give up too early, stick with it!

Trolling, stillfishing, casting lures or fly-fishing…the importance of accurate depth control and pre-sentation cannot be overstressed.

Just because you don't see them, doesn't mean they aren't there

Sometimes, no matter where you troll, the locator simply shows "no fish"! You would swear you were fishing in the Dead Sea! So you try deeper water, shallower water, opposite ends of the lake...still nothing! Don't give up...you may be in for the treat of your life.

This is a fairly common occurrence at higher-elevation lakes during early season, cold water angling, especially in those lakes with shallow water and/or gradual tapering shorelines. Until lakes begin to stratify and the thermocline of ideal temperature develops, fish will continue to prowl the shallows, the shoreline and the surface, with only occasional trips to deeper waters in search of food supplies.

Just because they are not visible on the locator, doesn't mean they are not there...fish can certainly be very close by. If fish are holding in shallow water or just below the surface in deeper water, they will rarely be seen on the locator, no matter how sensitive it is. As the boat approaches, fish

Lowrance locator: "No fish".

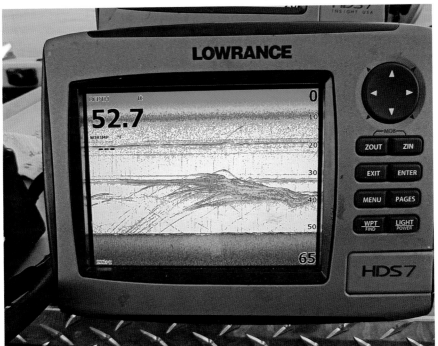

Marilyn with nice rainbow trout.

spook and tend to move out to the sides and scatter. This obviously places them outside the very limited range of the sonar signals of the locator. The cone-shaped signal from the locator is a visual image of a very small area beneath the boat. It might look like there are no fish, but they can definitely be there for the taking, if the troller can get the offering out to the side to intercept them.

Manufacturers of Electronic fish locators have consistently made huge strides over the years in improving their sonar equipment. These remarkable innovations in technology include side-locators, structure scan, bottom scan, forward scan...all unique tools that allow anglers to "see" directly forward, backward, underneath, and to the side of the boat trolling along, detecting fish holding or moving off.

Tackle manufacturers began to search for products to supplement the new technologies and a small "sideplaner" device evolved. This proven fish-catching tactic was originally utilized on big waters, using large side-trolling boards, but the smaller "in-line" sideplaner became increasingly popular with ultralight trollers. A sideplaner certainly assists in catching fish that have moved off to the sides and makes it possible for a troller to fish as far as 100 feet or more, to the side, while pulling lures 100 feet or further, behind the boat.

To catch bigger, smarter, more wary fish...disassociate terminal tackle from boat and engine noise. FOOL 'EM!

Sideplaners intercept fish that are spooked to the sides

This very effective method of trolling allows anglers to present terminal tackle to fish that are usually not seen on the fish locator. The "stealth" feature of a sideplaner enables an angler to fish in prime waters and to intercept many of the fish spooked as the boat passed by. A sideplaner assists the troller to cover more surface acres by placing line and terminal tackle up to 100 feet, or more, to the side of the boat. Another important bonus is the opportunity for the angler to send sideplaner and lure in tight to shore, in "big fish country", keeping the boat at a safe distance from shore without spooking fish. Sideplaners have made trolling with multiple lines much easier and provide anglers with the opportunity to catch more and bigger fish.

Several manufacturers offer small "in-line"—stays on your fishing line—sideplaners that are quite inexpensive. Small, lightweight and simple to use, these products have introduced the ultralight concept to sideplaning. Mini-planers, ranging from just five to eight inches in length, enable an angler to easily run lines to each side of the boat to get to places where fish are holding and feeding. The simplicity and ease of use of small sideplaners, plus their high-visibility colors, are popular with anglers.

In-line sideplaners.

Imagine an early morning on a favorite lake...sitting comfortably in the boat, quietly trolling 100 feet from shore in forty feet of water. The lure is slowly being trolled 90 feet to the side of the boat, five feet below the surface and only TEN feet from shore, in prime water! Simple and effective, sideplaners put offerings where the fish are, without spooking them!

More elaborate sideplaners are available, up to six-foot models, which allow lines to be let up to 150 feet to both sides of the boat. Four or more lines can be attached... let's see—eight lines on sideplaners...plus two out the back of the boat...totaling ten lines. That's certainly covering the water and one way to reach more fish – but might be a bit much!

Try experimenting with a sideplaner and an extra line or two. It takes coordination and a little getting used to, but is definitely worth it. The sideplaner gets reeled in with the fish, but the extra weight is worth it... the fish probably would not have been caught unless the lure was out there, attached to the sideplaner, away from the side of the boat.

Just a reminder...keep an eye on other trollers around you, or you'll catch more than you bargained for! Frankly, it's a good thing that most sideplaners come in highly visible colors.

Sideplaner in action.

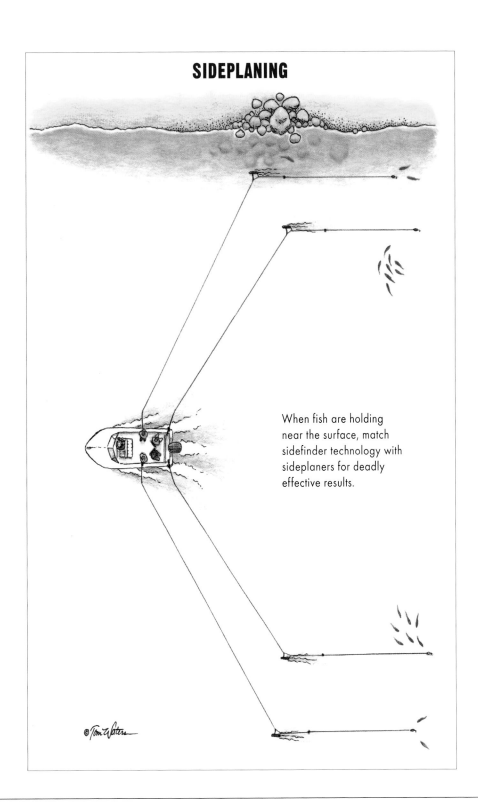

SIDEPLANING

When fish are holding near the surface, match sidefinder technology with sideplaners for deadly effective results.

©Tom Waters

8. VERTICAL HUNTING

Sometimes you have to work to catch fish

The electronic technology available today can certainly help unlock the combination to success. However, it is not always easy!

We taught ourselves a lesson years ago while fishing in what appeared to be perfect top-water conditions. We were trolling at a good speed, approximately one mph, and had set out lines 100 feet back. Ideal surface temperatures of 55-58 degrees indicated there should be good numbers of fish near the surface but they were small, few and far between. With an array of flashers, dodgers and small minnow-imitating lures, running from the surface down to fifteen feet, we trolled for several hours, but only a couple of small rainbow trout showed for the effort.

We continued to troll on top...until the locator indicated scattered fish, suspended in very deep 80 to 120 feet of water. It was time to pay closer attention to what the fish locator was signaling and time to "work" the electric downriggers...it was "technology time". To catch fish, would require working for them.

As each and every fish was marked on the fish locator, the downriggers were adjusted. Those fish were chased...wherever they were... the downriggers were raised and lowered to intercept fish from the surface down to 120 feet. By trolling offerings 100 feet behind the boat, we disassociated terminal tackle from the boat, engine and exhaust noises. Even more importantly, it allowed critical time to make necessary depth changes before the lures passed slightly above fish. The short time it took to adjust downrigger depths allowed the lures to pass very close to the holding fish.

These deeper fish were immediately found to be more active. They were bigger too, and obviously not recent planter trout. They could be clearly seen on the fish locator, streaking up from the depths to take a look at the offerings. These fish were holding and actively feeding, and chased trolled baits in the deeper water, striking with voracity. The success rate increased three-fold! In the next three hours, fifteen fish... rainbows and brown trout

Sep setting downrigger.

to four pounds, and landlocked king salmon to five pounds, were caught and released.

We refer to this constant adjusting technique as "vertical hunting". Since this first experience, the tactic has proven to work very successfully time after time. It is a practical approach and it works. By simply letting today's technology assist, fish are caught on days that other anglers may call "slow".

We have used a similar technique to catch kokanee salmon late in the season when they were tightly schooled and easy to see on the locator. We watched the locator closely as kokanee, in the eighteen to twenty inch range, followed offerings, without striking. The lures were set ten feet behind the downrigger ball, enabling us to turn tight and troll back through the schools. However, the kokanee would not bite. We decided

Guide Dale Daneman with kokanee in spawning mode.

to try to "tease" the kokanee to strike. The downriggers were raised and lowered rapidly, three to five feet each time, thereby changing the speed, depth, direction and action of the lures. This quickly provoked strikes from the irritated, or tempted, kokanee! "Teasing" has turned many a slow fishing day into fast action and productive angling.

"Vertical Hunting" and "Teasing"...just food for thought!

Gary Pilkington with the results of a good day of kokanee hunting.

Larger, more wary fish get big by being smart

Every day, first light and dusk are generally peak angling times. Dedicated anglers know that the "right" time always includes being on the water in the very early morning hours. Minnows, baitfish and game fish move to feeding areas and slowly, but methodically, create a food chain throughout the lake. As the first rays of light illuminate the sky, fish species become more active, searching out forage as well as eluding predators that may consider them a meal too. Dusk offers anglers another prime opportunity to intercept feeding fish and many times the evening bite far surpasses the morning bite.

However, do not be lulled into a morning/evening ritual. Fish will go on and off the bite several times each day and anglers can often miss prime time angling by restricting their activities to morning and evening fishing only.

In lakes where legal, fishing at night can often be the most productive time for big fish. Brown trout and rainbows drop their guard in the safety of darkness. Being primarily nocturnal feeders, bigger, more wary trout get big by being smart.

For years, we have kept a diary of our fishing excursions and this has proven invaluable in planning upcoming trips. Recurring entries clearly

Cliff Spediacci trolling on a foggy morning.

advise...NEVER, EVER fish on a full moon...obviously written after countless hours of angling frustration on the water. We have found that the best fishing occurs on a new or no-moon phase, or when the moon is so low on the horizon that it shines only a short period of time before disappearing. Out of necessity, however, we have not always been able to take our own advice.

What is it about a full moon that causes fishing to slow? There are many theories on the subject, including tides, gravitational pull of the earth and moon, specific feeding periods, and our favorite...the "bright full-moon, lit skies" theory. Basically, it goes like this. Fish see up. On bright moonlit nights, from below, trout can easily spot silhouettes of minnows or baitfish against the light surface. These easy pickings mean stuffed fish by dawn. By sunrise, the angler is fishing for trout that have been eating all night long. Make sense? It only figures that the best fishing would be on a new or no-moon...right? Maybe!

Generally, the period three days before a new moon and up to seven days afterward seems to produce the best action. We try to plan our trips accordingly with the use of a moon-phase calendar. To the contrary however, we have had phenomenal fishing success during bright-moon periods. How do you figure? Overall, there is certainly a correlation between a new moon and good fishing, but these periods too are affected by fluctuating barometric pressure and approaching storms or low pressure conditions.

Early morning and an icy downrigger.

Cold, wet and a 6-pound rainbow.

Certainly, variables such as these, plus cloudy skies and wind, have to be dealt with. Alone, or in combination, each will have an impact on angling success.

The single most important factor that decides the fate of a day of fishing, is the CHANGE IN BAROMETRIC PRESSURE. Rapidly changing barometric pressure often puts fish off the bite. Dropping barometric pressure signals a weather change or the arrival of a storm front. Rising pressure indicates the onset of high pressure or clearing weather. Quite often during these fluctuations, fish seem to get...lockjaw! When the barometric pressure bounces like a seismograph during an earthquake, select the days to go fishing very carefully. The day may look "fishable", but your quarry may ignore offerings for any number of reasons. Just let that pressure settle down and stabilize for a couple of days in a row, and angling becomes far more productive.

Anglers who can be flexible to plan trips conveniently around storms and changing barometric pressure will have better results. Unfortunately, storm fronts do not know or care about days off from work and anglers may be forced to fish on days when the pressure is dropping significantly. The day may look perfect initially, but as the front approaches from hundreds of miles away, the change in pressure is certainly detected by fish. They tend to shut down, possibly in anticipation of an impending storm.

It is frustrating, getting "skunked", and it happens to everyone. It is expensive, and even more importantly, uses up limited and valuable leisure time. Anglers want their chosen trips to be successful. The best way to do this is to let the high and low pressures stabilize, preferably letting a high settle in for a couple of days before heading out. If you can be flexible on dates, it pays off! Wait for the right day, when at least a couple of things are favorable, then give it your best shot. Under questionable conditions, troll deeper, and search for moving, actively feeding fish. When the pressure is dropping, fish will drop, too.

Let's take the subject one step further... a useful tool to help pinpoint the exact time of day to expect to find the best fishing and hunting periods, is available. In the "old" days, we checked with a small, thirty-two page paperback book, John Alden Knight's "Solunar Tables" which forecasts the

Cold sunrises.

daily feeding times of fish and game for every day of the year. Each day is broken down into two or three peak opportunity periods and by Region, it defines the window of maximum opportunity for anglers and hunters. This "Moon-Up/Moon Down" theory has been proven for years by outdoorsmen, both in the field and on the water.

These days, applications are available for Smart-phones, making data fingertip ready!

Similar to tide tables, periods when moon alignment is directly overhead or underfoot are spelled out. There are periods where for no particular reason, action breaks loose. We've all had those great days... is it luck, or just being persistent? Chances are, if you were to check out the tables, you would find a direct correlation between the action and the predicted peak periods. It may not always be right, but its accuracy has surprised us, as well as seasoned anglers.

We have been skeptical about the tables...but have used and verified them enough now to have reasonable confidence in their accuracy. They really do seem to work and if you are like us, you need all the help you can get! It just comes down to the fact that for one of a hundred reasons, you either catch fish, or you don't. And remember, just being there is half the fun and we have had plenty of great "fishing trips" when we've been skunked!

Timing is everything

Each year, normally during the early fall period, freshwater trout anglers anxiously and often impatiently await the arrival of the "turnover". It is no wonder! With turnover comes some of the best and possibly most exciting fishing opportunities of the year. Turnover, however, is a short-lived process and knowledgeable anglers know they must be ready to act.

Simply put...turnover is the process of "hypolimniation". It is that brief period of time brought on by the arrival of fall, when lake waters intermix and create the same temperature from top to bottom.

A combination of temperature change, wind and weather creates an upwelling inversion of water. This annual process consistently brings gamefish and bait to the surface at the same time. As the water and weather temperatures continue to cool, the nutrient and oxygen rich waters of the "thermocline" rise to the surface. This brings trout and salmon to the surface, too, where plankton, minnows and other naturally occurring meals are readily available. Generally, turnover conditions produce wide-open

Guide Doug Neal with turnover browns.

Sep having great fishing in the rain & wind.

bites when trout concentrate in the top twenty feet of water and larger holdover fish can be caught. As temperatures continue to drop, fishing will steadily improve, and then peak. The lake will restratify and trout and salmon, searching out their ideal temperature range, will subsequently be found at varying depths.

Starting first at higher elevation lakes, turnover will normally last from a few days to a few weeks before the arrival of winter. The water of the lake will slowly begin to restratify into the normal layers of the "epilimnium" (surface waters), "thermocline" (ideal temperature range), and "hypolimnium" (oxygen and nutrient-poor, deeper waters). Ideal temperatures, plus oxygenated and nutrient-rich waters provide "easy pickings" and puts turnover fish and anglers alike, in an aggressive frenzy. Fishing success will vary, eventually slowing down considerably as re-stratification takes place.

Check on favorite lakes to find out approximately when turnover will occur and plan trips accordingly. Marina operators and guides are well aware of conditions and will gladly share information. We always anxiously await the coming of turnover and the fall fishing season as it marks the beginning of great angling opportunities for trophy-sized fish. They are actively on the prowl, feeding frequently in an effort to build body fat to hold them through the cold winter months. This is the time that a properly presented bait or lure is likely to catch that one fish of a lifetime!

Trolling isn't always the answer!

As turnover occurs, trollers temporarily set aside the use of downriggers and electronics and begin "top-lining" for trout and freshwater salmon species. This long-line presentation of lures or trolled baits pulled shallow, about 100 feet behind the boat, is one of the best ways to enjoy the fight of a battling fish. If trolling lures, it is important they are about the same size as the minnows in the lake, generally about one inch long. White or pearl-colored lures are good producers because of their resemblance to minnows, the primary food source of trout. The addition of attractors such as flashers or dodgers will certainly enhance the presentation. Troll slowly, about one mph, off the main body of the lake, around points and drop-offs. Look for areas where there is less traffic and activity and therefore better fishing.

MATCH YOUR TACKLE TO THE TASK! Use a casting or spinning rod-and-reel combination loaded with six- to eight-pound-test line. A threaded nightcrawler or a lip-hooked minnow, where legal, trolled slowly behind small flashers will produce fish. Live-bait presentation is tricky…when you feel the bite, drop the rod tip back toward the fish and control the urge to set the hook. Let the fish hold on to the bait and the next time you feel movement, set the hook.

Nightcrawler.

There are a couple of other common techniques that shore fishermen or anglers still-fishing from a boat can consider. Try utilizing a sliding or slip bobber and ultralight tackle. A six- to seven-foot light-action spinning rod, equipped with a spinning reel with four- to eight-pound test line is perfect. When fish are suspended above the lake bottom or there are numerous snags and weed growth, bobber-stop devices enable the angler to set the exact depth of the offering.

The sliding-sinker method places the offering on or near the bottom of the lake. It presents bait in such a manner that fish do not detect, until it's too late, that it is attached to a rod and reel, and an angler. Cast out the desired distance that you think will intercept fish. With a spinning reel, leave the bail open so the line can move freely through the sliding sinker, allowing the fish to "hit and run", with

Andrew Erck "bankie" fishing.

the bait. After the bait has been taken and the fish begins to move off, slowly close the bail and wait for the line to tighten. Just as the rod begins to bend with the pull of the fish...set the hook. Just give a single, short, firm set. It is not necessary to "rip the lips" off the fish to set the hook!

Hunter Fletcher with a rainbow caught off breakwater.

Fly-fishing the shallows.

A threaded nightcrawler on a size 4 or 6 hook, or a dorsal-hooked minnow, where legal, simply cast out to drift is a deadly offering. While waiting for a hit, keep the bail open on the reel...a trout can feel minimal resistance as it takes the bait and hook. Wait to feel the pull of the fish before setting the hook. Handle the rod carefully and calmly. This technique allows the fish to move off with the bait without knowing the offering is attached to rod and reel. A premature set of the hook will only result in a missed fish. Control the excitement and wait until the rod bends...then set the hook...if you can wait that long!

In lakes where weeds grow heavily from the bottom, successful anglers use methods that float offerings above the weed beds. Nightcrawlers can be inflated with a worm-blower, available in most tackle shops. Another method, utilized for years, is to first thread a nightcrawler on the hook, and then attach a mini-marshmallow on the barb. This technique has definitely been refined with the introduction of floating baits, as the added buoyancy is all it takes to raise the offering several feet off the bottom and weed tops.

No matter how we personally feel, trolling is not always the answer to connecting with fish. Anglers should be prepared to still-fish or cast from boat or shore when circumstances dictate! With any of these "soft-bait" techniques, remember...do not set the hook too soon, or too hard...or you will soon be re-rigging your bait...instead of fighting a fish!

Slow trolling catches more fish

Best results are generally obtained trolling between one-half and 1-1/2 mph. Proper speed is very important for maximum lure action to entice fish to strike. Too slow...and lure action may be dead. Too fast...and the fish may not want to expend the energy to pursue it. Vary trolling speed, particularly when action is slow. Also, it's a good idea to give an occasional spurt of power to the engine. There are times that a cautious fish can be enticed to strike by the speeded up action of the lure.

Fish in the thermocline will be the most active, so an angler can afford to troll a little faster. If fishing above or below the thermocline, whether the temperature is warmer or cooler, troll slower. Fish in these areas are saving energy and will not waste it in a high-speed chase. Slow-trolled minnow-imitating lures can be deadly effective on foraging trout because they match the size and shape of natural food sources in the lake. On the other hand, when fishing is slow, search for that "impulse strike", by fast-trolling larger lures at two to four mph, top-water or on downriggers, with or without attractors.

Loaded downrigger.

"S" TROLLING PATTERN

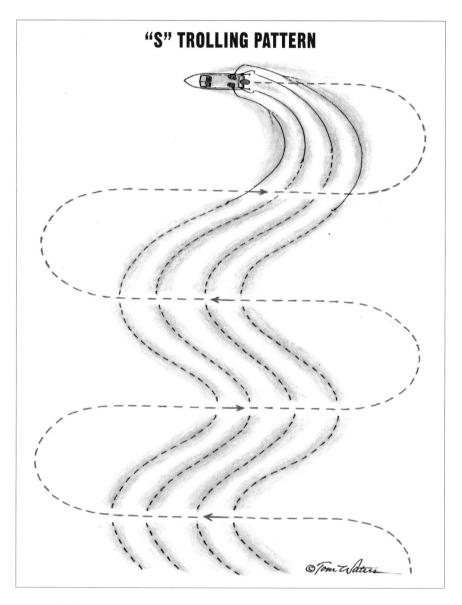

Troll in exaggerated "S" turns. Every experienced troller has seen it happen any number of times...make a turn and hook up a fish! Consider this...you are fishing with two rods and you make a turn. The lure on the inside rod slows down and DROPS deeper, while the lure on the outside rod speeds up and RISES to a shallower depth. The inside rod hooks a fish! The "S" turns allow the angler to cover not only more water, but the ability to place lures or bait at varying depths at once. It is a great tactic to catch fish because it automatically varies depth, speed and lure action.

Slow trolling is the way to go in cold weather.

Too many lines? In recent years, many states have initiated a "second rod" stamp to be added to a regular fishing license. When this happened in California... no problem, we thought. Instead of our usual two lines, we could now run four on the downriggers, all set at varying depths. This works fine when there are only two of us on board, but what happens when there are three or four anglers wanting to fish...SIX lines, or more? Maybe!

It is possible to easily troll five, six or more lines on the surface behind the boat, but making turns can be a lesson in weaving and braiding monofilament line. Therefore, it is important to stagger or vary the lengths of the lines so they do not overlap and tangle on turns. Put longer lines on the outside and shorter ones down the middle to reduce tangles and to allow a tighter turning radius. We have successfully trolled six or seven rods in the past without too much trouble, but you can bet we did not make any exaggerated "S" turns!

Traditionally, some of the largest trout of the year are caught during the cooler winter months. For cold-weather success, anglers need to adjust trolling techniques, especially speed. First of all, it is COLD! When water temperatures drop considerably, trout become increasingly lethargic. The impact of this cooling should not be taken lightly. As water temperatures drop below the ideal 52- to 58-degree range, trout and salmon will seek out shallower sun-warmed waters. Their metabolism, digestion and feeding patterns slow in an attempt to conserve energy. They are less likely to move any great distance and will not expend the energy needed to chase down their prey. Instead, they will wait in ambush for food that drifts or floats by within their attack range. It is the angler's job to attempt to provoke that impulse strike and to find the correct combination of vibration, color and most importantly, speed.

Light line and leader are a must

Keep it LIGHT, to enjoy the fight of the fish. Basically, four- to eight-pound test line on a six- to seven-foot medium-action rod will handle fish from one to ten pounds with ease.

Use high-quality, abrasion-resistant, small-diameter monofilament lines. When trolling, or still-fishing in freshwater lakes, correct line size depends on four main factors:

• Size and variety of game fish being targeted
• Casting or spinning rod and reel being used
• Pound test line recommended for the rod
• Most important, level of skill and experience of the angler

Most freshwater lakes will produce planted trout averaging one to two pounds in size. However, there is always the possibility of a trophy-sized specimen coming by and hammering the offering. Be prepared for such situations.

Many of the waters we troll produce trout from two to six pounds. Even so, we stick to lighter monofilaments. When using spinning equipment, we prefer six-pound test on our reels and four-pound leader of equal quality material. For level-wind or casting rods and reels, we upgrade to eight-pound test, with leaders of six-pound test. This allows us to troll faster with heavier trolling rigs or with larger lures that have greater resistance.

Sep with a good one on!

One of the disadvantages of using monofilament line is the "stretch factor", most lines rated at ten percent. With 150 feet of line out behind the boat…that translates into fifteen feet of stretch in the line…sometimes making it difficult to feel the initial strike.

The newer braided lines are all minimal stretch. Whereas monofilament can stretch up to ten percent before breaking, these lines have a maximum stretch of just two percent. With ultra-low stretch and virtually no memory or coiling, these lines deliver maximum sensitivity and firmer, faster hook-setting force. An angler can readily feel every head jerk and movement generated by a fish because of the minimum stretch feature of these lines.

A high-quality rod, offering good flexibility, matched with a quality reel equipped with a smooth-acting drag system can absorb a great deal of the shock when fighting even the largest of fish. It is possible to fight a fish that is considerably heavier than the line strength, if the drag on the reel is adjusted properly. This means…let the ROD and DRAG SYSTEM work for you. Set the drag properly and check periodically to be sure it has not changed. Keep in mind, there should be little, if any, sound of the drag working as you reel. The pump and reel technique, "pump up gently, reel down slowly", done correctly, creates very little sound and means it is being done right!

Another important consideration in selecting line strength is the size of the teeth of the fish you are after and the damage they could do to the leader. For instance, if hunting big trophy rainbow or brown trout, adjust upwards accordingly, such as to ten-pound test or more.

Anglers should not overlook the importance of low visibility when selecting fishing lines. Remember, fish look up and see objects, including fishing line, against a light surface. Fishing line colors of green and gray are the least visible to fish. Fluorescent clear blues are often highly visible and appear almost neon from below.

Leader Length

The appropriate leader length is unquestionably important. When trolling a bare lure, use at least a 36-inch leader and a swivel to help prevent line twist. However, all that changes when adding attractor flashers or dodgers to enhance the action and vibration of the lure.

Behind flashers, use a 12- to 24-inch leader, particularly when using a rubber snubber as a leader shock absorber. Many anglers prefer longer leaders, sometimes as much as 24-48 inches, when pulling flashers. Our feeling is that fish are attracted first to the churning blades, rather than the trailing lure. After all, the blades do create the fish-attracting vibrations and the lure should be enticingly close behind.

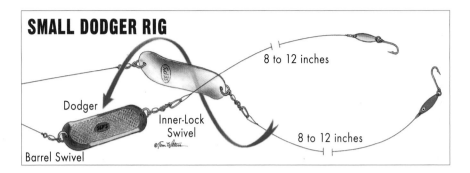

When using a small dodger to enhance the action and vibration of the lure, use just eight to twelve inches of leader. The formula for leader length is two to three times the length of the dodger. Using a four-inch dodger, the correct leader length would be eight to twelve inches. If the leader is too short, the lure will move so much that a fish may have a hard time catching it. If the leader length is too long, very little of the enhancing action of the dodger will be transmitted to the lure.

Preventing Line Twist

The initial opportunity to have line twist occurs when first spooling up. Line can twist as it comes off the spool and can become a problem even before getting to the water. Try turning the spool and feeding from the front, and the back, to determine which direction causes less twists as line goes on to the spool of the reel. Another trick to reduce line problems…once the reel is spooled-up, take it outside, and tie the loose end of the line to a fixed object. Walk backwards, keeping tension on the line. After letting out about fifty yards, pull on the line a bit to stretch it. This makes the line much easier to work with when fishing.

When using "casting" rods and reels, there is relatively little opportunity for line twist, one of the main reasons they are so popular with beginning and experienced anglers. "Spinning" reels are the real culprits, but their twists are generally operator caused errors.

Reeling Against the Drag

This is undoubtedly the most common way to get unwanted line twist. When retrieving offerings or fighting a fish, it is important to not reel "against the drag". If a fish is taking out line and you are reeling in at the same time, line twist is definitely being created. Each rotation reeled against the drag of a 5:1 ratio reel, will put five twists in the line.

Let the fish run when it is stripping line - do not reel against the drag. Using a "pump and reel" retrieval will help reduce the major cause of line twist. Pull back slowly with the rod, bringing in as much line as comfortably possible. Then, without lessening the pressure, reel in and take up line, while moving forward

with the rod. PUMP AND
REEL! If you can hear the
sound of the drag as you
reel, stop reeling. Use the
rod as leverage and as you
"pump and reel" correctly,
there will be very little
drag noise and very little
line twist.

Trolling too fast is
another easy way to create
problems. If trolling speed
is such that the lure, bait or
attractors rotate faster than
the swivels will allow…this
too will cause line twist.
A good idea is to use a
beaded chain swivel on the
line…this definitely helps
to minimize line twist.

Spinning reel and tangled lines.

Choose line carefully…and use quality, no matter how few times a year
you fish. Line connects you to your fish and wouldn't you be angry losing a "big
one" because line or leader broke? Knots are important too, and if you aren't
totally positive about the knots you have tied, re-do them! There are many
uncontrollable variables out there and you do not need to question the quality
of your line or knots while trolling.

Replace line and leader regularly and often. Sometimes replace line every
other day, depending upon how much time is spent on the water! Anglers should
check for nicks and abrasions when letting out line. Get in the habit of letting
the line slide through your fingers and feel for irregularities.

Here's a suggestion…after trolling most of the day, an angler might
notice that the line has become quite twisted. It is possible to undo many
of the twists rather easily. Slowly head across the water and take all the
hardware, including swivels, off the line. Let out line for 100 feet or so and
drag it along for several minutes. Bring it slowly back onto the reel. The
majority of the twists will be gone. This might save re-spooling and will
certainly save valuable fishing time in the long run.

Think about what is happening to lures or bait while trolling along. Line
strength, density, color and variety have been created for a multitude of
reasons. Try to utilize the correct application for your specific purpose. The
results will surely pay off, with more time in the water. After all, it is the
angler who has line in the water longer than another who catches more fish!

Fish are attracted first by vibrations

Every species of fish has an extended row of nerves that runs the length of its body. These nerve endings are referred to as the "lateral line sensors". To a fish, this is their sense of touch in the water. They can detect vibrations fifty feet or more away, depending upon weather and water conditions. In calm, undisturbed water, fish can "feel" further...and the troller has "attract-ability" from greater distances. In churned up water, fish often go into a feeding frenzy when minnows and baitfish become disoriented. This is why there is often an improved bite just as the wind begins to whip up the lake.

Marilyn with a great rainbow.

Fish are attracted first by the vibrations created from trolled offerings. In many cases, trolling is tremendously enhanced by the use of attractor blades, or flashers...and "flashers" is actually a misnomer! It is the "vibrations" created by the blades, not the "flashes", which initially attract fish. As fish are attracted and move nearer, they rely on their sense of sight, and move in closer when they spot the flashes. Their sense of smell then takes over as they key on bait or scented lures. Their eyesight is so poor that they do not detect colors until they are nearly upon the offerings.

Utilized for years, conventional, large flashers pull heavily on the rod, reel and line, and at times the angler can have a fish on and not even know it! Ultralight flashers were designed and developed for optimum fishing enjoyment. These small and lightweight trolling blades move through the water with little resistance and do not spook fish with excessive flashes and vibrations. They produce smaller vibrations when trolled slowly, similar to those of minnows and baitfish, attracting fish and enticing them to strike lures or bait. Manufacturers of ultralight flashers realized it is far more fun to play a fish with less drag on the line. "Feel the fight...it's ultralight" became a standard for trollers!

Additions to the tackle market include truly miniature and ultralight mini-micro flashers, designed to provide maximum vibrations from the lightest, most compact blades available. They have very little drag. At times, when just the slightest vibration or attraction is called for, when fish are spooked and hit very lightly, these smallest of flashers can be very effective. Plus, they're not

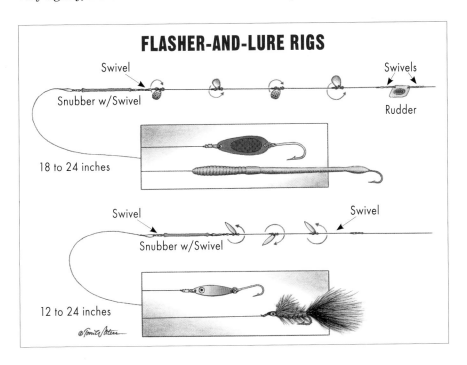

FLASHER-AND-LURE RIGS

Swivel

Swivels

Snubber w/Swivel

Rudder

18 to 24 inches

Swivel

Swivel

Snubber w/Swivel

12 to 24 inches

Banky Curtis and Larry Eng enjoying trolling.

just for trollers...this flasher system is also "castable" and can be utilized from shore by "bankies".

Which shape of blades produces the most vibrations as they are trolled through the water? The strongest vibrations, which can be felt farthest away by a fish's lateral line sensors, are created by the round "Colorado" shaped blades. "Tear-drop" or "Indiana" blades produce the next strongest vibrations. The weakest of the vibrations are created by the narrow "Willow-leaf" shaped blades. Which is the best to use? The one that is catching fish!

Flashers create vibrations but do little to enhance lure action. The dodger, an alternative attractor, creates vibration and more action, in addition to enhancing the movement of the lure. When trolled at slow speed, the dodger transmits a swimming, surging action to the lure or bait that many fish find irresistible. The side-to-side erratic motion produces action that causes strikes. Small, four and five inch and tear-drop shaped dodgers are lightweight and very effective. However, dodgers are also available in larger sizes and there are times that "bigger is better", and a troller should have a good selection in the tackle box to experiment when needed. Both types of products increase the action and/or vibrations of terminal offerings and definitely attract fish.

It is best to troll slowly and to diversify offerings, tactics and techniques. As your fishing day begins, vary equipment on your rods, utilizing either flashers or dodgers. After a fish or two is caught, re-rig to the most successful technique. When that method quits working, switch again.

Caught on a dodger.

Clarity of water assists the angler in determining which color of flashers or dodgers to use. A good general rule-of-thumb is to use silver flashers when water is relatively clear. In low light, deep or off-color water, use gold. However, these are just suggestions and results can be obtained

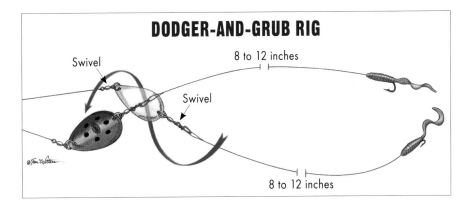

DODGER-AND-GRUB RIG

Swivel

8 to 12 inches

Swivel

8 to 12 inches

either way, perhaps just not as routinely. Some flashers have colored prism tape attached to the blades and this does enhance the flash. Bright, painted blades also have a spot in the troller's tackle box and are very effective when trolled in very clear water on bright days.

Dodgers come in assorted finishes: silver for clear water, gold or copper for dark or off-color water. Painted finishes and decorative colored prism tape can have major impact at various depths. Reds, oranges and silvers are best used near the surface, where sufficient lighting is present. The colors of gold, blue and green can be seen further underwater and in low light conditions. Chartreuse and pearl are versatile. Glow-in-the-dark dodgers are very effective when trolled at deeper depths.

What about attaching flashers to the downrigger ball, then trolling a bare lure or bait above? This is a relatively common technique, particularly with kokanee trollers, who find it very successful. It allows anglers to fish just a few feet behind the downrigger ball, and is generally not recommended for trout trolling. The flashers, usually made with larger blades, are attached to the downrigger weight, eliminating the "in-line" aspect. This reduces the drag even more. Simply let out five to ten feet of line and connect to the release, about three feet above the weight and flashers. The vibrations of the flashers attract and excite fish, which then hopefully, hit the lure in the process.

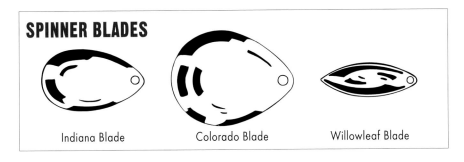

SPINNER BLADES

Indiana Blade   Colorado Blade   Willowleaf Blade

Depth helps to determine which color to use

Do fish see color? Do they select food sources of one color over other colors? Studies have been conducted over the years and fish apparently have the cells and pigments needed to be able to see color, but they, like us, do not see colors well in low light conditions. It is known they can distinguish different shades of color and the most involved research we have read states that blue and green are strong favorites.

Some basic guidelines regarding color choices:

• On bright sun-shiny days with clear water conditions, use silver lures
• On dark or overcast days, gold is recommended
• Brightly painted lures are by far the most visible
• Colors of red, orange and pink, sunrise and sunset colors, are best used near the surface in the top thirty feet or so, depending on water clarity and available light
• White and shades of green and blue are effective in deeper, darker water where there is less light penetration
• Chartreuse and pearl are consistent producers, no matter at what depth.

It is action and vibration that initially attract fish. When slow trolling at speeds of one half to one mph, use lures that imitate the minnows and bait-

Variety and sizes for ultralight trolling.

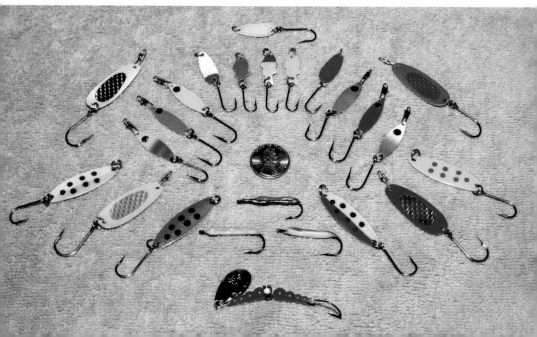

fish in the lake. Fish are limited in what they eat by the size of their mouths. Larger trout with larger mouths can take much larger food sizes than small trout can. Think about this when selecting which lure to use. Check the action of the lure by observing it on the line, in the water alongside the boat before letting it out all the way. Ensure the action is smooth and correct. Some lures require "tuning" or bending and even a swivel can sometimes alter the performance or action of the lure.

Check the movement of threaded nightcrawlers, minnows, lures or trolled flies and grubs to ensure they run true and "slither" through the water without rolling or wobbling unnaturally, or twisting the line. Slight adjustments in hook direction can generally correct irregular movements. A worm-threader or a threading needle can simplify rigging.

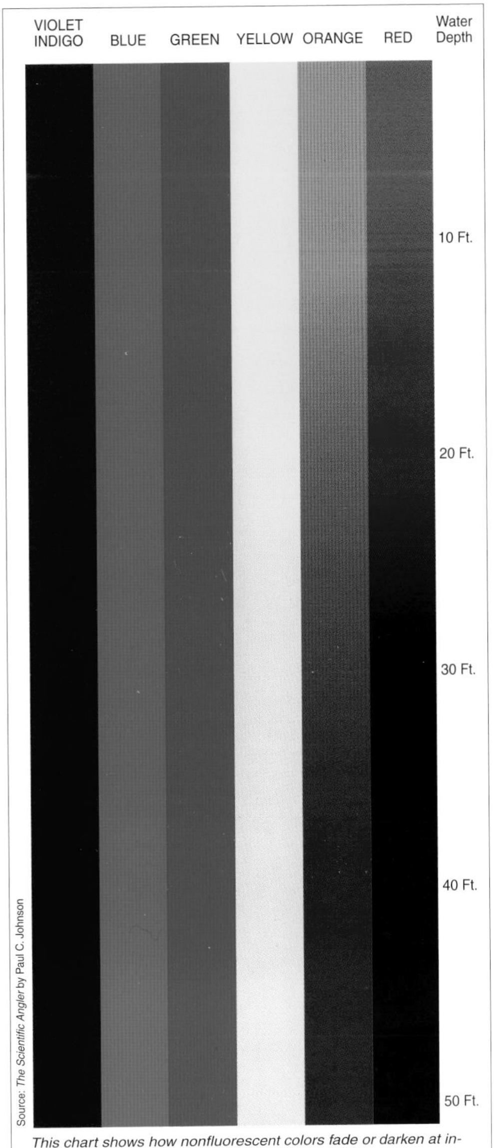

Minnow-imitating, lightweight, flutter-type lures offer maximum action and vibration when trolled at low

| VIOLET INDIGO | BLUE | GREEN | YELLOW | ORANGE | RED | Water Depth |

Source: The Scientific Angler by Paul C. Johnson

This chart shows how nonfluorescent colors fade or darken at increasing depths in clear water. A red lure 20 feet down, for example, appears nearly black. Fluorescent colors persist much deeper.

speeds. Their appearance, presentation and action make them very effective. Lures in various colors with prism tape provide a scale-like appearance that matches natural food sources. Lures available in chrome, gold plate, copper or brightly painted finishes provide high visibility under water.

When fishing for kokanee, tip the barb of the hook with white corn... not yellow...WHITE! No one really knows why it works, but this "magic"

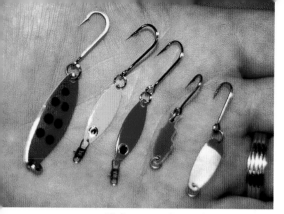

Fish-attracting colors.

can make or break a kokanee fishing day. Some anglers say it works because it is a maggot imitation, while others think it creates a scent path, or it looks or smells like plankton, primary food source of the kokanee.

Scents can effectively be mixed into the corn, to create "cocktails" that some anglers say, no fish can refuse! Anglers mix corn with anise, minnow or crawfish scents to create their own fish attracting concoctions, sometimes even using food coloring to add to the mix. Artificial corn products, floating baits and maggot imitations come in pre-scented and various colored applications which provide the variety that some kokanee anglers search for. Anglers do catch kokanee by placing a small piece of nightcrawler on the hook, but undoubtedly the angler using white corn or some variation of it, will out-fish them all!

Finding the correct combination of action, vibration and colors of lures is not easy and do not be reluctant to change lures. Experiment until the combination is unlocked – that's really part of the fun of kokanee catching!

Sep and Shooter trolling lures.

There is no doubt that scents work!

Awide variety of manufactured scents or attractants, each with a distinctive odor and individual success rate, are available to sport fishermen. It is confirmed that trout and salmon can sense small amounts of chemicals in large bodies of water.

Fish attractants do three things:

- Most important, they mask human scent. Oils and smells produced naturally by human bodies can repel fish and cause them not to strike. Trout and salmon species have a keen sense of smell and may turn away from lures that carry normal human odors, or unnatural scents created by tobacco, gasoline, cologne, perfume, strong soap, etc.
- Attractants create "scent paths" that entice fish to follow a lure or bait. A trolling angler can create an attractant trail that prowling fish may intercept and follow, thinking they are closing in on an easy meal.
- Because of the natural smell and taste of the scented lure or bait, a fish may hit and hold on to it longer, providing additional seconds for the angler to "stick" the fish and set the hook.

There are many scents available to sport fishermen.

Scents work!

There is no doubt that scents work. On most days, using scents can improve angling action dramatically. At times, we have trolled awhile, without catching a fish and then realized we had not applied scent. After applying an attractant, a fish has been caught almost immediately! Is this just dumb luck or the effect of the scent just used? We prefer to think it is the attractant!

Always go fishing with a wide variety of "smells". They come in many "flavors", including crayfish, anchovy, shrimp, sardine, herring, nightcrawler, anise, corn, garlic, and more. Attractants come in many forms and can be applied by spraying on, pouring on, wiping on, rubbing on, etc.

Consistent success is found using biogradable odiforous "jellys" and "butters" with a wide variety of natural or artificial bait odors which work on all baits and lures. Other widely used products are the real thing ground up – trout, anchovy, nightcrawler, crawfish, shad, etc! Easy-to-use sprays also work well. An application of any of these scent products will last for several hours. As a matter of fact, they last so well that it is recommended wiping lures clean before placing them back into the tackle box.

John Eagleton with a nice kokanee.

There are also products that remove scents instead of creating them. Most odor eliminators are biodegradable and easy to use on hands and skin. They can be used on fishing and hunting equipment, cutting boards, counter tops, etc. We have the scents, smells and flavors to entice fish, plus methods of removing scents from our hands... but do we have the "sense" to use them?

Draggin' flies works!

When fall "turnover" is complete and surface waters have cooled considerably, fish of all species begin to feed heavily in preparation for the harsh winter months ahead. Instinctively, feeding and building fat reserves, "energy", becomes the top priority of the fish. Trout and salmon will pursue a wide variety of food sources but it is the minnow or baitfish that offers the most energy per meal...and fish know it.

When presented properly, one of the most realistic minnow imitations is the trolling fly. Available in a wide variety of fish-attracting colors and designs, trolling flies that imitate minnows, or leeches, emergers and other natural baits are excellent producers. Used in place of lures, spoons or nightcrawlers, flies are proven producers because they move realistically, imitating natural food sources.

Trolling flies are effective, versatile and fun. They can be trolled top-line by themselves, but the angler must create the fish-attracting action, by methodically and consistently twitching or pumping the rod tip to pass action to the fly. An erratic figure-eight design, drawn with the rod tip also creates a most effective attractor. Repeating and varying this action creates the realistic motion the fish is looking for before it strikes.

Flies can be effectively trolled behind flashers for spectacular results at times. They can also be deadly effective when top-lined behind small dodgers. The side-to-side action and vibration of the dodger imparts an enticing swimming, surging action to the fly that attracts fish. The addition of a dodger also adds weight, which takes the offering down slightly deeper. To get even more depth, use downriggers, diving planes or weights, but the reaction by the fly is solely dependent upon the flasher or dodger leading the way.

Trolling flies are extremely effective when top-lined with sideplaners. The preferred technique is to let line and trolling fly out approximately 100 feet

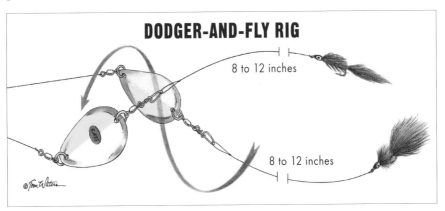

DODGER-AND-FLY RIG

8 to 12 inches

8 to 12 inches

Sep and a rainbow caught on a fly.

behind the boat, then to connect the line to the sideplaner. Let the sideplaner run 40-50 feet, or more, to the side of the boat. This gets the offering out to the side, where fish holding near the surface have moved, as the boat passed over them. Sideplaners also enable anglers to get into those close-to-shore, hard-to-get-to spots where fish are cruising in search of a meal.

Far more important though, is the natural action transmitted to the fly as the sideplaner moves and surges through and across the surface of the water. The sideplaner works especially well when trolled in water that has a slight chop or wave action...surging across the surface, the sideplaner naturally imparts the necessary fish attracting action to the fly.

Paul Hendrickson with a rainbow caught trolling a fly.

When selecting a color of fly to use, attempt to imitate the natural food sources found in the lake. Blacks, browns and cinnamon resemble leeches... whites and grays look like minnows, and olives and black/olives bear a startling resemblance to emergers - dragonfly and damselfly nymphs. The vibrant, hot colors of chartreuse, pink, orange and purple are in a class of their own...and often get a reaction when nothing else is working.

The next time you wonder which lure to use, try draggin' flies...they work!

You may never use a nightcrawler again!

Small two- and three-inch curl-tail grubs, normally used for panfish or bass fishing, offer anglers a realistic-looking imitation of natural food sources when trolled.

Whether imitating minnows, leeches or aquatic insect life or simple nightcrawlers or worms, properly presented grubs are excellent attractors. Available in a wide variety of colors, grubs move through the water in an enticing, vibrating manner that attracts fish to strike. Much like trolling with flies, running grubs behind flashers, dodgers or with sideplaners will increase their effectiveness. Match the color, size and speed of natural food sources available and positive results and hookups will follow.

White grubs imitate minnows. Black is best for freshwater leeches, brown for nightcrawlers or worms and green for minnows and aquatic insects. The

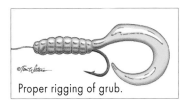

Proper rigging of grub.

brighter, more vibrant colors like hot pink, bright orange, chartreuse and purple are also productive because of their visibility in a wide variety of depths and light conditions.

You may never use a nightcrawler again! Black and brown grubs are perfect imitations for nightcrawlers.

Once you have tried using grubs and experienced the results, you will soon experiment with various colors, trolling speeds, the use of downriggers and sideplaners, plus the addition of scents. The tackle box will definitely contain a selection of grubs!

Effective? Deadly effective…just give them a chance!

Allan Bonslett's trophy rainbow using an orange grub.

Speciacci's boatload trolling grubs.

No need to rip the lips

Warning! Watching too many bass-fishing television shows before going trolling for trout or kokanee is not a good idea!

Many times, an angler will lose a fish because the hook was set with enough force to pull a marlin out of the water! Remember, for the most part, the trout and salmon species talked about here are small fish in the 12- to 20-inch range. Even the bigger ones do not need a major hook-set...it is not necessary to slam the hook home. All that is required is tightening the line... just cinching it up, plus a light tug, will generally do the trick. Actually, most of the time, especially when trolling, the fish will do it for you!

Using a rubber "snubber", a small five- to six-inch tube with coiled line inside, is beneficial when trolling flashers. Many anglers hook and successfully land more trout and salmon using a snubber as it helps to ensure the hook-set is not too hard. A snubber gives the line just the right amount of elasticity at the onset of the strike, to keep the line from snapping. It also acts as a shock absorber during the fight. When using flashers and a nightcrawler or grub, or flashers and a lure, attach the snubber just behind the flashers, then clip the leader on to the other end of the snubber.

Sep with a nice kokanee.

To vary the action to the lure or bait, attach a small dodger instead of flashers. Kokanee trollers find the use of dodgers to be particularly effective. A dodger will give a surging, swimming action to the offering and a different technique is utilized. A snubber is not recommended for use with a dodger because it deadens the action of the dodger as it is transmitted to the lure.

Keep in mind, when a kokanee is hooked-up, do not horse it in. Use "finesse". The mouth of a kokanee is very soft and its intense struggle requires the angler to "baby" it to the net. If drag is set too tight or excessive pressure is applied during the fight, the paper-thin mouth will often tear and the fish will escape.

When a kokanee gets close to the boat, it really starts acting "salmon-like". A kokanee will jump, tail-walk and basically go crazy, and the closer it gets to the boat, the harder it fights. This definitely requires the angler to be gentle and very careful...maintain steady pressure, be patient and above all, enjoy the fight.

By the way, more kokanee are lost right at the boat as the angler attempts to net it! Consider using a very long-handled net...eight feet of reach often spells the difference between a netted or a lost fish.

Rainbow in the net.

Wendy Carrington nets Sep's fish.

Certainly an angler's two most important tools

Rods

Manufacturers produce both "spinning" and "casting" style rods in a vast array of models and sizes designed for every type of fishing imaginable. The objective is to select the exact rod, and reel, for the type of fishing planned. Freshwater trollers should have at least two, if not three, rod-and-reel combinations to handle all trolling needs…ultralight 4- to 6-pound test line…medium 6- to 10-pound-test line…heavy 8- to 12-pound-test line.

From a ridiculously low price to unbelievably expensive, rods are made and designed for the basic beginner to the discriminating professional. Do yourself a favor…test some of the higher quality rods available the next time the opportunity presents itself. Whether that moment occurs on the water using a friend's rod, or in the aisles of a sporting goods store, give it a wiggle…handle it. Better yet, if at all possible, fight a fish with it. Then make your decision.

Spinning rods and reels are called such because of the method in which line unfurls from the reel. Spinning rods are designed with larger guides at the bottom, tapering in size to the smallest at the tip. The guides gradually straighten out the unfurling line, enabling the angler to cast greater distances than with level-wind models.

Many an angler has been satisfied for years with a current fishing "pole", without realizing what reduced weight and better action can do to improve

Hot action.

Paying attention to the rod.

enjoyment of the fight of the fish. The many and varied fishing rod manufacturers offer anglers state-of-the-art technological improvements in their products and continue to design, develop and promote new and better equipment.

Several years ago, we fished with friends at a favorite lake. They had recently purchased a big boat, equipped with all the toys and whistles trollers enjoy utilizing. We were into fish and watched as our lady friend caught several in a row, reeling them in quite proficiently. When the rod nearest her husband dipped, and because he was busy with a downrigger, she took the rod. She played the fish and brought it to the net, with a big smile on her face! She had used his rod for the first time and although she had been quite critical of the cost when he purchased it, she realized the difference was definitely worth it. The next time we fished together, all rods on their boat were the same!

We regularly take three rods each when trout or salmon trolling... two spinning rods and one level-wind or casting rod. This provides choices depending on size of fish, trolling depth, water conditions and other variables. Also, by pre-rigging, we always have a rod ready to go, should there be a big-fish line break, a hang-up, or any other traumatic event!

Reels

The quality of the reel is very important but how much to spend depends upon the angler. A high-quality reel with smooth drag systems can last a lifetime if taken care of properly. Look for reels with at least three ball bearings and sufficient spool size to hold a quantity of line in the pound test required. A spinning reel should hold at least 100 yards of line. Most casting reels are capable of holding more than enough line. Knowing the difference between "spinning" and "casting" rods makes a big difference in matching reels to rods. Designed to suit every possible need and price range, the selections are wide and varied.

Recently, at a favorite tackle shop, a customer in line explained to the salesperson that he wanted a good rod-and-reel combination to

Lowrance locator with structure, lines and fish.

fish for EVERYTHING from crappie to striped bass! Unfortunately, there is no combo that offers great feel and action that will cover all species! It is necessary for an angler to own at least a couple of combinations for fishing for multiple species of game fish.

Many anglers prefer level-wind or casting reels because they find them easier to handle and operate than spinning reels. Also, trolling with casting reels means greatly reduced line twist.

Spinning reels, often called "eggbeaters", require slightly more experience and coordination to use. Often preferred for control when fighting a fish, a spinning reel can also be an angler's worst nightmare. Reeling against the drag when fighting a fish or retrieving line, can cause excessive line twist. Spinning reels come in both front and rear drag models. Performance wise, the front drag is preferred because of the larger surface area of the drag washers that allow line to move off the reel smoothly without surging or stressing it. Conversely, rear drag reels have smaller surface areas and are not as effective, especially over the long haul.

For Rod Browning technique pays off!

Maintain a selection of sizes of reels in both spinning and casting types. Basic rod, reel and line combinations are capable of handling fish in excess of ten pounds. The "smaller the better" works for most trolling, but there are certainly times when there is a need to match tackle to the task. The ultralight designs create greater action...that equate to more FUN when fighting fish.

After all, just like with terminal tackle... match rod and reel, to the task.

The most planted game fish

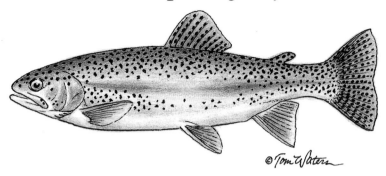

© Tom Waters

Rainbow trout are found as lake and stream trout and as anadromous or ocean-migrating, stream-spawning species, known as steelhead. Rainbows are second only to cutthroat in diversity of subspecies and range. Historically, that range included the Pacific Coast drainages from California to Alaska.

The leaping ability of the rainbow is what angler's dreams are made of. A hooked rainbow can leap from the water in an aerial display a dozen times or more, before reluctantly coming to the net. Rainbows readily strike offerings and can be caught on spinners, flies, grubs and a wide variety of baits ranging from nightcrawlers to minnows. Their primary diet consists mainly of insects, plankton, crustaceans, leeches, fish eggs and small minnows.

Rainbows have short heads and silver bodies with numerous small black spots along the sides. Most also display an iridescent pink stripe down the side that gives them the name "rainbow". The backs are dark green and sometimes nearly black in color. Pelvic and anal fins are tipped with white and numerous small black spots adorn the dorsal and caudal fins. Due to the extensive diversity of conditions found in different lakes and streams, this species can display a wide variety of colors, shapes and sizes.

Growth is highly variable, depending on the habitat and available food supplies. Stream rainbows grow to about one pound in four years. However, in large bodies of water where food is plentiful, rainbows can early reach ten pounds in the same amount of time.

Classified as spring spawners, they may spawn as early as December or as late as June, depending upon the weather and elevation.

Rainbows are the most planted game fish in the Western States. They are raised in hatcheries and planted as adults and sub-adults in lakes, rivers and streams throughout the West.

Identified by the red streak on each side of the head

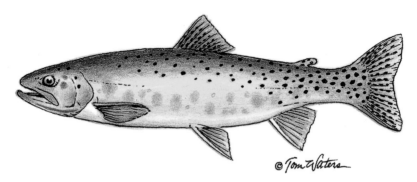

© Tom Waters

Historically, the cutthroat had perhaps the largest range of any North American trout and the Lahontan cutthroat was the largest size of any trout. Habitat loss and competition with rainbow trout, which is stocked heavily in much of the cutthroat's range, has diminished its range and population. The four recognized sub-species are: Coastal, West Slope, Lahontan and the Yellowstone cutthroat.

Cutthroat trout are a medium to small-sized salmonid with widely varying colorations and markings. Typically, they are light olive on the back and upper body, with silver to blush colored sides spotted with black dots. All species of cutthroat have a streak of red on each side of the lower jaw, therefore the name "cutthroat". They have larger mouths and smaller scales on the body than rainbow trout and often cross breed with rainbow trout species, which has had detrimental effects on the pure strains of cutthroat.

Depending on stream flow and water temperature, cutthroat spawn in the spring, normally from April through July. In lakes as the cutts prepare to spawn, they move in closer to shore and become easily susceptible to offerings. Cutts are often found holding near the bottom, waiting for an easy meal to swim by. Strong vibrations generated by flashers and dodgers will attract them to lures, flies or properly presented grubs.

As with other species of trout, it is best to disassociate terminal tackle from boat and engine noise. Sideplaners can be used to intercept fish holding tight to shore in very shallow water. Downriggers will assist in intercepting fish holding near the bottom in deeper water. Just about any type of lure is effective and the size of the lure should be appropriate for the size of the quarry. Five- to ten-pound cutthroat will feed on fish from two inches to twelve inches in length so an angler should be prepared with a full arsenal of lures.

You don't catch big browns...you fool 'em!

©Tom Waters

The brown trout is identified by the olive brown color with pronounced red spots surrounded by a bluish halo, found mainly on the sides of the fish from head to tail. The tail is nearly square with little or no visible spots.

Anglers respect brown trout because they are so difficult to catch. They are aggressive and can attain sizes of up to forty pounds, depending upon environment and food sources. They are elusive: they do not like sunlight, preferring shaded areas, weeds, crevices and deep water. They may be well out in the lake, following schools of kokanee or feeding on rainbow trout, but they

Mary Lowe with a nice brown trout.

Andrew Erck and his brown trout.

are nocturnal feeders and can be found early in the morning and late in the evening, roaming shorelines. Natural food sources such as minnows, leeches, crayfish and insects round out their diet and primary inlets and outlets often hold browns waiting for a meal to drift by. For an angler to intercept a brown, you have to think like they do. Big browns get big by being smart!

An opportunity to catch big browns is in the spring, when run-off and abundant food supplies spark feeding instincts. Also, in the fall, as the spawning cycle begins, browns drop their guard and become more aggressive and susceptible to offerings. They can be seen swirling on the surface or may hold at depths that require the use of downriggers. Trolling offers the best opportunity for success by covering as much water as possible, putting offerings ranging from flashers and nightcrawlers to trolling flies, minnow-imitating lures or big plugs into varying environments. Fast trolling, at one to four miles per hour, hoping for an impulse strike, is what makes brown trout fishing exciting. However, big fish are also wrestled to the net each year by surprised fishermen, working from the shoreline or anchored boats.

Whatever choice, fast or slow, deep or shallow, it is all in the presentation. Never has the right pound test line and leader been more important. Terminal tackle and lures must be disassociated from boat and engine noise – troll 100 to 150 feet behind the boat as these fish can be spooked by anything less than natural presentation.

Don't expect to catch a trophy each time - patience and persistence will pay off, but the key is luck and skill! The thrill of catching, and releasing, a monster brown trout is an exhilarating experience.

Freshwater Sockeyes...Blue-Backs...Silver Bullets

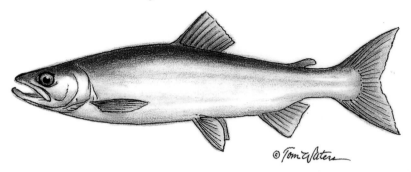

© Tom Waters

Oncorhynchus nerka is the scientific name and means "hooked nose of flowing waters". Kokanee are silver in color with dotted backs and tail and most average from 12-18 inches in length. Size is totally dependent upon the size of the impoundment, available nutrition and competition in the lake. Kokanee are the landlocked - non-anadromous - form of sockeye salmon. They are not a trout but belong to the same family as the trout, and are found in some of the same areas. Kokanee feed almost exclusively on plankton and zooplankton.

Kokanee turn bright red during spawning periods and males produce a pronounced hooked jaw. Generally, in the fall of their third or fourth year of life, both male and female kokanee spawn and die shortly after.

For pure fight and tenacity, the kokanee is a much-respected game fish. To do battle requires specialized tackle, some skill, luck, finesse and often a great deal of patience! Often, kokanee trolling can turn into a "fire-drill"...they often travel in schools, and fast hook-ups can occur at any time, followed by total inactivity...until the bite starts up again.

A wide variety of specialized tactics and techniques will work on catching kokanee. Trolling devices such as flashers create vibrations that attract this inquisitive fish. Behind flashers, anglers run 14-18 inches of leader to small, brightly colored lures tipped with white corn or small pieces of nightcrawler. A rubber "snubber" is helpful to protect leader and to keep the hook from ripping out of the kokanee's soft mouth.

For variation, dodgers add enticing surging, swimming action to the lures. To maximize action of the dodger, the leader to the trailing lure should be about four times the length of the dodger. Small lightweight, flutter-type lures work best. Some trollers attach a set of flashers to the downrigger ball for extra fish-attracting vibration...it works!

Kokanee catching is a matter of doing EVERYTHING right and it is essential to match your tackle to the task.

An exciting and tasty addition to any lake

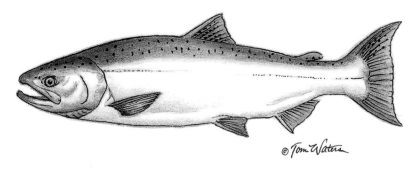

© Tom Waters

Numerous lakes and reservoirs throughout the West are planted annually with king salmon fingerlings or smolts. The addition of kings to freshwater lakes has created an additional tier for fishing, as kings occupy deeper, cooler water than most other game fish.

An exciting and tasty addition to any lake, king salmon are tireless battlers with exceptional growth rates in bodies of water where ample food supplies are available. Meat-eaters that require a great deal of protein, they thrive in lakes with rich populations of pond smelt, threadfin shad or other non-gamefish minnow species. They can range in size from six inches to upwards of 20 pounds-plus in some lakes. A short three- to four-year growth period precedes the annual fall spawn.

Bart Bonfantini, Jr. conqueres the king.

Kings are often found in schools and when one is caught, it is likely more will be caught if the angler stays with the school. Fish-catching techniques are similar to those used for trout but trolling depths will be slightly deeper. Flashers and nightcrawlers or grubs work well as do dodgers and minnow-imitating lures. When using lures, tip the hook with a piece of nightcrawler to increase odds of success. Big lures, smeared with scent, work underwater wonders when trolled as fast as two to three miles per hour.

A.k.a., Lake Trout

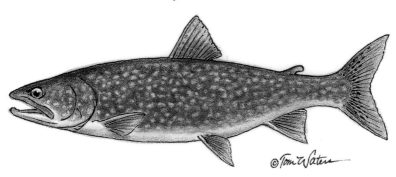

The lake trout is greenish to olive in color and has spots and marbling distributed on fins, tail and sides and to some extent, on its unique forked tail.

Mackinaw are actually a member of the char family. They are generally found in deep, cold waters that often hold populations of rainbow trout, brown trout and kokanee salmon. Mainly a forage fish, they feed heavily on small baitfish, planter trout or non-gamefish species like squawfish, suckers, smelt or sculpins. In some lakes, out of necessity, they feed almost exclusively on plankton, insects or crustaceans. Macks require cold, well-oxygenated water and in summer move to depths of 50-100 feet, and deeper. In spring and fall, they can be found at depths of 20 feet or less but their preferred water temperature range is from 40 to 52 degrees.

Lake trout are slow growing, especially in very cold-water environments and they live a long time, sometimes reaching an age of 40 years. In cold-water climates, where "thaw-out" may last only 100 days, it may take 15 years for a mack to reach two pounds. Most macks are caught in the two-to 20-pound range but they will often grow in excess of 30 pounds or more.

Fishing for mackinaw requires specialized tackle and techniques. A quality locator capable of deepwater reading, is essential. Downriggers are important and depending upon the depths where macks are hanging, it may be necessary to use wire line. Terminal gear varies greatly from large plugs to dodgers and threaded minnow set-ups, where legal. Minnow-imitating lures in rainbow, pearl or kokanee color patterns can also be trolled effectively behind flashers or dodgers.

Lake trout wage strong, determined underwater battles, fighting, as many guides say, with their "shoulders" with short forceful runs and give-and-take pulls. Most macks are taken by trolling with spoons or minnow-imitating lures attached to wire line or downriggers.

27. STATE-OF-THE-ART TECHNOLOGY

A mix of electronics and technology – tools to catch fish

Anglers and boaters live in a world of change with amazing innovations and constant upgrades of technology to keep them on the "cutting edge". Electronics, fish locators, Global Positioning Systems, mapping, waypoints, auto-pilot steering systems, bottom contours, electric trolling motors, side-scanning…it's amazing – the tools we have for the simple act of "fishing"!

Sorting through the array of available fishing tools is like wandering through a maze of gadgets and gimmicks designed to catch as many fishermen as fish. New technology and ideas bring additional products to the retail market every year. There are consistently new tools that anglers can use to improve their fishing, the quality of their fishing, and most important, enjoyment of that fishing.

Many anglers scrimp and save to purchase the latest in a fish locator and after doing their due diligence and checking reviews, purchase the unit of their dreams with all the bells and whistles imaginable…until next year! Now, unlike years past, when your unit needs to be replaced because it's out of date, or too old…or newer models with newer applications are on the market, you don't need to buy a new one. Many major manufacturers of electronic locators allow you to upgrade your unit by simply downloading the latest technology via the Internet, or by the local dealer. This extends the life of and improves the capabilities of your existing locator, and saves money too. You can afford the latest NEW GENERATION of electronic products! Lowrance Electronics recently announced a new HDS GEN2 system - hard to imagine improvements after that - but you can bet there will be!

After 40 years of fishing and testing, we give you our proven choices of trolling equipment currently rigged on our JETCRAFT 2025 Stingray:

Lowrance Electronics

We're believers in Lowrance Electronics. Our boat is rigged with an HDS-10 High Definition System…the best! Innovative…State-of-the-Art…and dependable.

Lowrance's finest combo GPS chartplotter/fishfinder, this unit has it all - everything you could possibly need in a locator! With a stunning 10-inch high-definition screen, the HDS-10 reveals every last detail in low and bright light situations. The HDS-10 has full mapping, tracking, recording and so much more, with built-in GPS antenna and structure scan plus an expandable system that ties your entire boat operation into the single HDS unit. It is hard to imagine where technology will take us in the next 20 years!

Lowrance.

Hand-Held GPS Units

An ever-growing number of both fresh and saltwater anglers have learned the benefits of Global Positioning System – GPS – navigational receivers. Recent innovations have given anglers incredible clarity and detail of both land elevation and contours. The units clearly map lake and river bottoms with contours and depth too...in addition to all the trails, roads, lakes, streams, rivers and more...lots more. Unbelievable, and hard to think that it will get even better!

These small, lightweight units have become an important tool for both tournament and recreational anglers alike. Anglers who find prime fishing spots such as drop-offs, reefs, humps and springs, can permanently and accurately record that location in the GPS unit memory. This enables an angler to return to the exact spot to intercept feeding fish at that same location, time after time. Or perhaps...you and a buddy are on a trip with really hot action...and you wonder if you can find that spot again...simply punch a way-point into your hand-held GPS device...and that fishing hole is electronically marked...forever! You will always be able to find it!

These units are so accurate that some tournament and professional anglers now scout lakes by airplane and store the way-point settings of prime fish-holding locations in river inlets, outlets, springs, channels, etc. There are many excellent portable hand-held units available and we choose to use Lowrance full-color models.

GPS.

Some of the Smart Phones have GPS applications that do similar tasks, but with far less detail. We suggest you not use them for on the water navigation, but they can help you find your way back to a favorite spot...if you have reception. Download Lowrance aka NAVIONICS which has a great application for I-Phones, with GPS and full mapping features. What will they think of next?

Minn Kota

The Terrova is built for power to stand up to anything you encounter and when equipped with an IP-ilot remote control, speed and steering control is effortless. Spend your time fishing instead of steering and correcting! The autopilot corrects speed and direction for wind, waves and current as you troll. It's changed the way we

Terrova Freshwater Bow-Mount Trolling Motor with IPILOT 24.

fish, forever - we would not consider going trolling these days without our Terrova.

It is perhaps one of the prime tools of our arsenal, giving us access to fish that most anglers never see or troll near. We use it exclusively when trolling. Basically noise free as we move through deep or shallow water undetected, stealth gives us the ability to pull sideplaners or lines directly behind our boat into shallows without the noise of a gas engine spooking the fish. Our Terrova easily gives us eight hours of continuous trolling without a recharge - it has plenty of power and a fantastic auto-pilot control system with solid and dependable performance.

We also installed the Johnson Outdoors Minn Kota battery-charging system. We have five batteries rigged to handle all tasks on board...four Scotty electric downriggers, a 100-pound thrust Terrova 80, Lowrance HDS-10 locator, VHF radio, lighting and too many accessories to list...all tied together through one charging system. The best part - just plug it in when you return and it's ready to go again the next morning, fully charged! A big plus: how much quieter it is on the water without the gas engine chugging along! Even more entertaining is what you hear other boats say as they pass...kinda interesting!

Scotty Downriggers

Our new Jetcraft Discovery 2025 Stingray is rigged with the newest from Scotty. The new Scotty's are the fastest downriggers on the market and are perfect for shallow and deep-water trolling applications. All-new designs feature illuminated digital counters, unbeatable pulling power, adjustable rocket launcher rod holders, and a clutch brake with the largest braking surface in the industry, allowing for ultra fast speeds. They are impressive!

Scotty downriggers.

All models of Scotty downriggers are spooled with Scotty HP Downrigger stainless steel wire, but, anglers can upgrade to the latest in silent "no-hum" DYNEEMA. This line is similar to many of the super lines on the market today and is line with 200 pound test, very small diameter, less drag and subsequent "blow-back". This simple change from stainless steel to super line eliminates that annoying wire hum as you troll along on your favorite water. With wire we always wondered...do the fish feel the noise or vibration as it moves through the water...are we scaring fish with the noise? The answer is YES. Less noise in and on the water...means you catch more fish...most of the time!

Jetcraft

We would be remiss if we didn't provide highlights of our Jetcraft Discovery 2025 Stingray! Technological improvements have revolutionized boat construction, especially in the aluminum welded fishing boats category. Our Stingray is built for enhanced hard-core boating performance with a versatile partial hard top, sliding windows and canvas front closure. It is 20-feet 3-inches long, with a beam of 90 inches and an impressive 32 inch rail

Jetcraft.

height. We have swivel seats, tons of storage, full electronic features, stainless steel rails, diamond deck trim and an EZ Loader trailer that makes launching effortless. Our boat is comfortable and safe, and it looks terrific on the water too!

You can be assured that technology will continue to provide anglers with bigger and better "toys". There is no end to what can be imagined, dreamed, invented or built, and anglers will always seek new and innovative products in their quest for assistance in locating and catching fish!

Freshwater techniques – just as successful in saltwater

While saltwater trolling is not the main topic of this book, it is important to note that the trolling techniques discussed will assist in targeting and catching more fish in the saltwater environment too. The important consideration is the species being pursued. Is the quarry a tight schooling fish like rockfish, or is it ocean king salmon that are likely to be scattered across a broad area?

While trolling might not be as effective for tightly schooled fish, freshwater trolling techniques are equally effective in saltwater on most species, especially those varieties that suspend in the water column and feed on smaller baitfish. Ocean king salmon are simply the saltwater cousins of landlocked freshwater kings so it is important to upgrade tackle and terminal presentations to handle fish in excess of ten to 60 pounds plus. They will be found from the surface to 300 feet deep during their foray along the California/Oregon coast where they feed until returning to their original spawning grounds to spawn, die and continue the cycle of the salmon.

Dawn Suliak with a halibut caught in Alaska.

Because of the "bigger" water in the ocean, an angler might find the need to speed up to initiate a strike or to find fish willing to strike. It is important to increase the size of the downrigger weight. The 6- to 10-pounder used on lakes for trout and salmon species, should be upgraded to 10 to 15 pounds. An ocean angler is impacted by tides, currents, trolling speed, wind and other variables that can cause "blow-back" and inaccurate depth presentations. Using a heavier downrigger weight in saltwater will keep lines straight down at the proper depth and there will be less blow-back and fewer subsequent inaccuracies in trolling depth.

In Northern California, many professional guides and charter boat captains troll for halibut in the ocean and San Francisco Bay, utilizing techniques in much the same way as lake trollers. The only difference is that halibut

Shirley Spediacci with a striped bass.

trollers always keep terminal tackle near the bottom... their flasher/anchovy rigs dancing a foot or so off the bottom...above halibut waiting just under the sand to attack anything and call it lunch.

Trolling is universal – freshwater or saltwater. Anglers cover as many surface acres as possible, searching the varying depths looking for "marks"

Wendy Carrington with a halibut.

on the locator. When fish are identified, we adjust our depths and presentations and speed up or slow down actions, depending on the aggressiveness of the gamefish pursued. Ocean salmon are the primary target of saltwater trollers on the West Coast, requiring a simple upgrade to tackle for the battle. Heavier rod and reel, heavier line, heavier downrigger weights, lures, hooks and a BIGGER NET is about all an angler should need!

Tried-and-true freshwater trolling techniques are just as successful when trolling in saltwater!

From a long-running
popular segment on the radio show!

These are "CLUES" that relate to every angler on the water...helpful hints, suggestions, pointers, time-savers, ways to stay out of trouble, and more. Check them out...does it sound like someone you know?

Poaching Fish

Many fishermen still have a tendency to put their "keepers" on stringers... then dangle them over the side of the boat. In cool fall and winter conditions, this is probably an adequate way of keeping fish fresh. However, in bright sunlight and very warm temperatures, it doesn't take long to "poach" the catch.

If planning to keep fish, it is best to "dispatch" kill immediately. As fish struggle and die on stringers or flop in empty ice chests, they build up lactic acid that begins to break down the muscles. The meat gets very mushy very quickly. A swift "BONK" on the head, a quick "wood shampoo" is the fastest way to dispatch the catch. Put the fish on ice immediately and keep it cold. This will slow the natural breakdown of the meat and will keep it firmer.

If you like fresh, clean tasting, firm textured, delicious fish – always have an ice-filled cooler available and toss your catch into it right away!

Releasing Fish

To "catch and release" fish...act quickly, once the fish is at the boat! The fish is tired and stressed after the fight, and if you want photos, always keep the camera handy and ready to shoot. You have about as much time as you can hold your breath to get the photo and unhook the fish. That's about a minute, which is plenty if you're prepared...not very long, if you're fumbling around.

To help that fish survive, keep it in the water and try not to wipe off the protective slime that helps to keep the fish alive. Wet your hands and hold the fish just behind its head, right over its gill covers. Don't touch the gills or eyes...and don't squeeze its stomach.

Pulling on the hook, just sinks it in deeper. Grab the eye of the hook with needle-nose pliers and try to push it back into the fish's mouth. Once the barbed end is free, you can slide the hook out. If the lifesaving technique appears to be failing, do not waste the fish. BONK it, and put on ice to enjoy later on!

Launching

Launching a boat on a ramp requires practice. To learn, first take the boat and trailer to an empty parking lot and practice without an audience!

When backing down the ramp, remember...the trailer turns in the direction opposite to the direction you turn the steering wheel. To adjust for this, place your hand on the bottom of the steering wheel. When you turn the wheel to the right, the trailer will turn to the right. Roll down your window and watch what is happening!

One more thing...be very sure the drain plug has been placed into the boat!

Launch Ramp Courtesy

Time on the ramp should be very limited, which means...be ready. Be efficient, prompt and thoughtful! All the guys lined up behind you are anxious to get into the water too. Your turn comes up when your vehicle is next in line, proceeding to the ramp, whether you are launching, or taking your boat off the water.

Prepare before backing your vehicle and boat trailer down the ramp. There is nothing worse than waiting for the loading of rods, coolers, kids, dogs, chairs...or whatever, into the boat...on the launch ramp.

In the dark, turn headlights OFF on your vehicle so the next guy lining up isn't disoriented in the glare of lights. A driver is unable to safely back up when there are headlights in the rear-view mirror.

Once launched, get the boat moved as far along the docks as possible, making room for others behind. Get your vehicle parked correctly, in an assigned space, and hurry back to the boat. Get it started and get out of the way!

Be aware of surroundings, think about what you are doing, and instead of creating RAMP RAGE, your efforts will be appreciated.

Be A Good Sport

Know the rules and regulations and practice courtesy and safety on the water. Troll far enough away from anchored or still-fishing anglers to give them room to cast. If anchored, leave enough room between boats to allow trollers to motor through. Courtesy dictates that you should keep at least a 30- to 50-yard buffer zone to avoid crossing over or tangling lines with fellow anglers. Be particularly careful about wakes when passing through anchored boats...slow down!

Don't follow another troller too closely and avoid crossing too close to the bow. Always envision where your lure is – if you drag line and lure in front of another troller's boat, chances are you will hook the line or downriggers.

Be observant, pay attention to what is happening, in your boat and in the water around you. Think about what you are doing and get into the rhythm or pathway of others around you.

Exhibiting common sense and common courtesy will make adventures on the water far more enjoyable.

Boating Safety

Most boating fatalities each year involve fishermen and almost all of these could have been avoided by paying attention to a few boating issues.

All individuals in the boat should wear a lifejacket. New advanced styles are available that are comfortable and not bulky, and should be worn at all times.

Make sure the number of passengers does not exceed limitations of the boat. Keep everyone seated and if a person stands up to fight a fish, make sure the others don't rock the boat. Passengers should not block your view – be aware of what is ahead. Drive the boat at a safe speed, slow down for turns, do not create hazardous wakes and be careful crossing wakes. Be extra cautious in unfamiliar waters.

Last, but not least...boating and alcohol do not mix!

On The Water

Going fishing soon? No matter how experienced you think you are, do keep these thoughts in mind.

Tell someone where you are going...who is with you and how long you think you will be gone.

Check all boat equipment...engine, fuel supply, lights, wiring, etc.

Keep an eye on the weather. Sudden wind shifts, dark clouds or choppy water generally mean something is coming.

Watch your fish locator...it tells you much, particularly water depth and temperature and keep the GPS and cell phone handy.

Be careful, and wear your lifejacket!

Weather By Numbers

Wind speed plus swell...the way to stay out of trouble. Follow this guideline when waters and seas are marginal and good action is enticing you to fish... maybe when you should not.

It works like this – add the wind speed in knots and the swell height. If it equals more than 20, then it is not SMALL BOAT weather.

For instance, wind speed at 15-knots with 8-foot swell...15 + 8 equals 23. That is alright for party boats but for the average 20-foot boat, it is uncomfortable. With 10 knots, with the same 8-foot swell – that is 18, which is fishable...and most important – SAFE.

With a larger boat the numbers can go up to 25, but it starts getting really rough. Always wear a lifejacket!

Don't Get Lost

Weather conditions can change quickly and if you're participating in outdoor activities, you need to make sure you don't get lost...out in the wilderness, or on the water.

Know where you are at all times and the best way to do this involves using a map and compass. Don't leave home without these tools and be familiar with them. Your sense of direction is not nearly as dependable as a compass, so always look for landmarks and look behind as well as in front. Pay attention to everything around you!

GPS, Global Positioning System – the most important navigational aid ever! It is truly state-of-the-art and our most useful tool. However, when night falls or reception weakens or batteries die...trouble could be ahead.

Tell others where you are going and always be prepared. Carry extra clothing and food...plus the cell phone...in the event you do get off the beaten track. Don't take chances, it's just not worth it!

Carbon Monoxide

Whatever type of fishing you do, be well prepared for the elements. When weather patterns are unstable, the day could start with sunshine, but by mid-afternoon, you could be in the middle of a major storm.

If your boat has zip-in windows and doors, make sure there is enough ventilation inside that cocoon. When you close yourself in, remember to have an adequate air supply. Carbon monoxide from the boat motor can creep in undetected and can quickly fill the space. It will kill you!

It's odorless, colorless, tasteless and non-irritating. It is very dangerous, causing headache, nausea, weakness and dizziness and in some cases, is thought to be seasickness. Fresh air is important...it can save your life!

Instructions

Got a new locator, downriggers, some far-out tackle, accessories, or a new reel? Have you tried to use something and it just won't work...until you take a moment to read and follow instructions!

Manufacturers provide directions, drawings, videos and internet details to help customers utilize their products to maximum potential. To get the most out of any item is to know how it works...and that applies to something as simple as a lure, or as complex as electronic technology.

Look at the packaging, read the back side before you toss it in the trash, or read the instruction booklet BEFORE, not after, attempting to use the item. Hang on to the information for awhile in case a refresher course is needed!

Tipping The Guide

If you have the opportunity to hire a guide and go fishing...do it!

It's a great experience, having the guide do all the work, while you get the glory. You pay the guide...but it is also good manners to tip...so how much?

An average, nice trip with a guide with basic knowledge, warrants ten percent. Two guys on a $300 deal, would tip $30, or $15 each.

A good trip, a guide with decent knowledge, who knows more than you do and has good equipment...would tip 15 to 20 percent. That $300 trip...around $50.

A great day, an excellent time, a guide who knows what he's doing and gives results...justifies a 25 percent tip...that is $75 to $100.

Take that trip, on the water or in the field...a professional guide saves you countless hours of frustration. Enjoy the trip, and the memories...and tip accordingly!

Cigarette Butts

Anglers who smoke are intelligent, caring, knowledgeable people who refuse to believe the daily news. It's an obnoxious habit, but...

Butts, as in cigarettes and cigars, do not mix well with water. When a leftover butt is casually tossed into the lake or stream, it will not dissolve. Chances are a fish will come along and slurp it up...butts do not digest in the stomach...so the fish will die.

The answer? A caring person will smoke cigarettes downwind of everyone and will carry a small metal container with cover for butt storage. The butts don't go into the water and there is no smell on board the boat. It's an offensive habit, but we welcome our friends to go fishing with us anyway!

Safety Chains

You see it on the highway often...some guy just lost his boat while towing it. Not only did he create a major traffic jam...the folks passing this mess don't think highly of this "sportsman".

The hookup between vehicle and boat trailer requires safety chains. This is the use of a hook, with spring-loaded clip. Not an ordinary "S" hook, which can bounce free of the hitch.

Twist the chains before connecting to the hitch. This shortens them and puts the hook under pressure, with less chance of bouncing loose. Also, crossing chains makes a cradle for the tongue, if the ball and tongue do happen to disconnect on a bumpy road. And, do not forget to use tie-downs!

Trailer Bearings

Another calamity seen on the side of the road often is a boat trailer with a wheel jacked up, requiring help. If you tow your boat everywhere; on roads, highways, on gravel and dusty roads, check wheel bearings and hubs regularly and OFTEN. It is a good idea to check the bearings thoroughly one year, and replace them every other year.

Keep bearings full, not overloaded, with good marine-grade grease. Carry an extra set, just in case, plus the tools you might need, including a grease gun.

Also, visually inspect trailer wheels and tires, tighten lug nuts and the trailer hitch ball, plus make sure the winch is working smoothly.

One bad experience and you will definitely be prepared to handle boat-trailer emergencies in the future. Sitting on the side of the road is not pleasant!

Tire Pressure

Get into the habit of checking tire pressure – on your vehicle, and boat trailer!

Tires are considered your lifeline, yet tire failure is the cause of most accidents, especially when towing a boat or trailer. Under-inflation is obvious, because excessive sidewall flexing creates overheating, causing blow-outs. Keep an eye on and maintain proper tire pressure!

Tandem axles on trailers do not steer. Their wheels flex and loosen more than single-axle trailers, and they need to be tightened frequently, using a torque wrench.

Tire pressure...check often!

Protect Belongings

Most folks you meet in the Great Outdoors are nice, honest, dependable...right? Well, maybe not everybody fits that description. Do not get burned by burglars!

Protect vehicles, boats and belongings by taking precautions when you leave them in remote areas, or even in launch ramp parking. Don't leave stuff in plain view of passersby. Hide gear in the trunk, under the seats or cover with clothes. Roll up windows and always lock vehicles and campers. Use good locks on boat engines and boat trailers. An alarm is a practical addition and even out in the boonies, the shriek will send most burglars running.

Keep track of fishing rods and tackle boxes and do not leave them in tempting locations. Sad to say...trust no one...not everybody is a nice guy!

Keep It Clean

Recently on a fishing trip, we trolled into a long scenic arm of the lake to enjoy the pristine area.

Another time, we took a 4-wheel quad run into the hills.

Why is it everywhere we go, we find...glistening in the sun...garbage! Beer and soda cans, glass and plastic bottles, Styrofoam, plus all sorts of other debris.

Who are the disrespectful people who do this? What would possess anyone to toss a can, or bottle, or leave trash? And another thing – broken glass everywhere!

Don't be a thoughtless, littering slob. When you leave, there should be no sign you have been there. Pick it up, pack it home, dispose of it properly and do your bit to make this world one we all enjoy!

Check out what we do!

SEP'S OUTDOORS, INC. is a media-related company, interacting with the outdoors in the fishing and hunting community. Sep and Marilyn Hendrickson manufactured the SEP'S line of ultralight trolling equipment until a few years ago when they sold the company. In "retirement" they have developed other avenues of communication...in radio and video.

Sep & Marilyn in the studio.

Sep is the host of "California Sportsmen", an award-winning radio show, broadcast weekly on Saturday mornings from 6:00 – 8:00 AM on KHTK 1140AM, Sacramento, CA. This popular show is designed to keep listeners up to speed on current outdoor action in Northern California, other locations throughout the West, and popular locales. Sep's on-the-scene, on-location interviews with professional fishing and hunting captains and guides highlight their expertise and knowledge. The show covers "issues" and current affairs, and interviews with outdoor writers, conservation organizations, magazine editors, resort owners, and more, providing insight into where and when to go and how to do it...a total package, bringing the best in outdoor entertainment!

Sep's other show, "Ultimate Bass", the only all-bass radio show in the country, is hosted by Bass Pro Kent Brown...also on Saturday mornings, 5:00-6:00 AM, on KHTK 1140AM.

"California Sportsmen" and "Ultimate Bass" radio shows are live-streamed through seps.com, ultimatebassradio.com, are archived and MP3 and iPOD downloadable.

SEP'S OUTDOORS website...seps.com...highlights the activities of Sep and Marilyn and their Brittanys, Jackson and Shooter, their friends and acquaintances. A link to the radio shows is also available on the website.

We enjoy all we do!

As all anglers know, catching fish remains a matter of being in the right place at the right time, at the right depth, at the right speed, with the right lure, in the right color, with the correct action and proper presentation!

There are times when looking at a fish becomes an almost religious experience!

As technology continues to improve, taking advantage of what is available will certainly help anglers catch more fish. We need all the help we can get and we know that good equipment, plus good luck, equals good fishing.

The main thing is to get out there and do it! No matter how successful the angler, the privilege of being in the great outdoors is in itself a reward... and a FISH IN THE NET IS A FINE BONUS! Take care of our resource by keeping only what is needed or used...release the rest to grow and provide anticipation and excitement for anglers to come.

Practice C.P.R. "catch, photograph and release"! There are times that looking at that fish in the net becomes an almost religious experience. Having a photograph can bring back a happy memory!

We are so glad to be a part of this wonderful sport of FISHING!

SEP AND MARILYN HENDRICKSON, SEP'S OUTDOORS, INC., are outdoor enthusiasts and writers/photographers who enjoy trolling for trophy trout, kokanee and landlocked king salmon. Sep is host of "California Sportsmen", an award-winning weekly radio show, broadcast on Saturday mornings, 6:00-8:00 AM on KHTK 1140AM, Sacramento, CA. He is a popular seminar speaker, providing trolling tips in an informative and humorous manner, and is often requested to act as MC at various functions. Sep is Executive Director, Marilyn is Vice-President, of California Inland Fisheries Foundation, Inc., a non-profit organization dedicated to improving freshwater angling in California.